The Development of University-Based Entrepreneurship Ecosystems

The Development of University-Based Entrepreneurship Ecosystems

Global Practices

Edited by

Michael L. Fetters
Babson College, USA

Patricia G. Greene
Babson College, USA

Mark P. Rice
Worcester Polytechnic Institute, USA

and

John Sibley Butler
The University of Texas at Austin and IC² Institute, USA

Edward Elgar
Cheltenham, UK • Northampton, MA, USA

Published by
Edward Elgar Publishing Limited
The Lypiatts
15 Lansdown Road
Cheltenham
Glos GL50 2JA
UK

Edward Elgar Publishing, Inc.
William Pratt House
9 Dewey Court
Northampton
Massachusetts 01060
USA

Reprinted 2016

A catalogue record for this book
is available from the British Library

Library of Congress Control Number: 2010922131

ISBN 978 1 84980 263 5

Printed and bound in Great Britain by the CPI Group (UK) Ltd

Contents

Figures

Tables

Boxes

Contributors

Jose Manuel Aguirre Guillén, Director, Technology Park, Instituto Tecnológico y de Estudios Superiores de Monterrey.

Kathleen Allen, Director, USC Marshall Center for Technology Commercialization and Professor, Lloyd Grief Center for Entrepreneurial Studies, University of Southern California.

John Sibley Butler, Herb Kelleher Chair in Entrepreneurship, McCombs School of Business, The University of Texas at Austin and Director, IC^2 Institute.

Janice Byrne, Research Assistant, EM Lyon Business School.

Alain Fayolle, Professor of Entrepreneurship, Director of Entrepreneurship Research Center, EM Lyon Business School.

Michael L. Fetters, Walter Carpenter Distinguished Professor, Babson College.

Arturo Torres García, Associated Vice-President for Entrepreneurship, Instituto Tecnológico y de Estudios Superiores de Monterrey.

Karla Giordano, Director of Business Incubators and Accelerators, Instituto Tecnológico y de Estudios Superiores de Monterrey.

Patricia G. Greene, F.W. Olin Distinguished Chair in Entrepreneurship, Babson College.

Yuen-Ping Ho, Research Fellow, NUS Entrepreneurship Centre, National University of Singapore.

Mark Lieberman, Assistant Professor of Clinical Entrepreneurship, Lloyd Greif Center for Entrepreneurial Studies, University of Southern California.

Mark P. Rice, Dean, School of Business, Worcester Polytechnic Institute, USA

Annette Singh, Research Fellow, NUS Entrepreneurship Centre, National University of Singapore.

Poh-Kam Wong, Professor, NUS Business School and Director, NUS Entrepreneurship Centre, National University of Singapore.

Acknowledgments

A book project of this magnitude and complexity requires the contributions of many people. We would like to acknowledge and thank them all. Our collaborating authors – all busy leaders of university-based entrepreneurship ecosystems (U-BEEs) – delivered thorough and thoroughly inspiring chapters. Thank you Jose Manuel Aguirre Guillén, Kathleen Allen, Janice Byrne, Alain Fayolle, Arturo Torres García, Karla Giordano, Yuen-Ping Ho, Mark Lieberman, Annette Singh and Poh-Kam Wong. Lindsay Evans, our writing and editing partner, did a phenomenal job, improving the language and formatting of the chapters while also retaining the flavors of the contributing authors. Thank you, Lindsay, and also Deepti Tomar who provided vital support in formatting references, tables and figures. The two host universities of the editors – Babson College and The University of Texas at Austin – provided vital support. The IC² Institute and the McCombs School of Business at The University of Texas at Austin hosted our workshop in May 2009, and Babson College provided research funds. Thank you to Alan Sturmer, senior acquisitions editor, Edward Elgar Publishing, for his support. We salute all the sponsors, champions and leaders of U-BEEs worldwide and hope that our book helps you enhance and accelerate your U-BEE development process.

Finally, and most importantly, we would like to thank our families for their love, understanding and support:

Michael Fetters	Linda, Seth and Zach
Mark Rice	Lisa, Lia, Mark and Katie
Patricia Greene	Ken, Kenny, Kevin and Shaun
John Butler	Rosemary Griffey Butler.

1. University-based entrepreneurship ecosystems: framing the discussion

Patricia G. Greene, Mark P. Rice and Michael L. Fetters

INTRODUCTION

Economic failures and social distress drive an intensified interest in entrepreneurial activities around the world as entrepreneurship is increasingly looked at as one of the answers to the world's woes. Academic institutions vary greatly in their responses to the demand for entrepreneurship education. This book builds on the premise that the most impactful approaches to entrepreneurship are those that go beyond the start of a small business to include both an entrepreneurial mindset and a skill set for entrepreneurs, resource providers, suppliers, customers and policy makers. The desired end result from this broad collection of stakeholders is to create an environment, an entrepreneurship ecosystem, in which there can be an increase in entrepreneurial spirit, skills and support systems that together result in an increase in economic and social benefits.

Many academic institutions are looking for guidance on how to frame, design, launch and sustain their efforts in the area of entrepreneurship. This book provides pathways to the development of university-based entrepreneurship ecosystems (U-BEEs), recognizing the wide range of missions, contexts and resource sets available to different schools in different places. With an appreciation for this range, we affirm that there are many approaches that might work. Our chosen task was to present an overview of quite different schools and their entrepreneurship ecosystems, along with a description of the components of each ecosystem and their development processes and the identification of their success factors.

The institutions whose programs had been identified as exemplary were invited to attend a conference co-sponsored by Babson College and the IC² Institute held in May 2009 in the McCombs School of Business, at The University of Texas at Austin. The team from each school was asked to present a case study of their U-BEE, including:

- An evolution timeline highlighting the critical stages of development.
- Outcome measures of success tracked during development.
- Ecosystem benefits experienced across campus and beyond.
- Key success factors of the launch of entrepreneurship and the ecosystem.
- Key success factors for sustaining the U-BEE.
- Current and emerging challenges.

The one-day workshop featured presentations and in-depth discussions and debates about the similarities and differences of the programs. The authors of the chapters that arose from this workshop came from schools in Asia, Europe, Latin America and the United States. In their case studies they extracted lessons learned across contexts, countries and institutions to create a model that allows entrepreneurship education to have impact across campus and beyond campus borders.

The U-BEEs described in this book are multidimensional enterprises that support entrepreneurship development through a variety of initiatives related to teaching, research and outreach. The associated activities include, but are not limited to, such things as the collection of entrepreneurship course offerings, the integration of entrepreneurship in core requirements, case writing, the development of innovative pedagogies and teaching materials, student-led conferences, alumni entrepreneurs as faculty and speakers, on-campus new venture development, educational extensions of entrepreneurship education into areas like family enterprises, social entrepreneurship and corporate innovation, funded entrepreneurship research that crosses disciplinary boundaries, and outreach initiatives that build a meta-ecosystem connecting entrepreneurs and support organizations (other universities, government agencies, non-governmental organizations (NGOs) and business entities). In short, a U-BEE is integrated and comprehensive, connects teaching, research and outreach, and is woven into the fabric of the entire university and its extended community for the purpose of fostering entrepreneurial thought and action throughout the system.

Generalizing from a case study, or even six case studies, must be approached cautiously. Therefore we start this book with a short overview of related theoretical approaches to suggest frameworks our readers might find useful in understanding and considering the application of the recommendations shared by our contributing authors. We move from there to a brief introduction of each of the case studies and conclude this introduction with a statement of objectives. We then present case studies of six exemplars: Babson College, EM Lyon, University of Southern California (USC), The University of Texas at Austin, Tecnológico de Monterrey, and the National University of Singapore (NUS). The book concludes with a reflection on lessons learned, including patterns of evolution, key success factors and straightforward recommendations that we believe will guide other universities seeking to develop and sustain entrepreneurship ecosystems. The development of U-BEEs offers an opportunity for educational institutions to establish a culture of creativity, innovation and action, as well as to become a force in stimulating entrepreneurship activity regionally, nationally and internationally.

THEORETICAL APPROACHES

There are many ways to approach the theoretical deliberation of the intersection of entrepreneurship and regional economic development, even given the added consideration of the role of the university. Prior to 1965 the research on relationships between organizations was considered underdeveloped, even described as 'of little beauty or power' (Stinchcombe 1965), with the notable exception of relationships creating and supporting markets and governments. Questions about how businesses related to each other or to other types of organizations were rarely asked and even more rarely answered. However, along with the subject of markets and governments, ethnic entrepreneurship emerged as an early way of looking at how individuals, businesses and other community and religious organizations worked together to build businesses and ultimately communities (Greene and Butler 1996). These business systems of ethnic entrepreneurship, ecosystems in their own right, included an array of support and resources. Much of this type of discussion came under the framework of either classic or truncated-middleman minority theory (Butler 1991).

Population ecology and institutional theory approaches gave additional support to the fundamental importance of examining entrepreneurial evolution as a system (Zacharakis et al. 2003; Neck et al. 1999; Spilling 1996). For the purposes of this book we follow a theoretical framework that focuses on the ecosystem itself for Part I (Babson College, EM Lyon and USC) because these schools exemplify ecosystems that were motivated by the desire to provide students entrepreneurship education that directly supports entrepreneurial activities both pre- and post-graduation. In Part II (The University of Texas at Austin, Technológico de Monterrey and the National University of Singapore), we add the dimension of technology transfer and commercialization, introduced by Butler in Chapter 5 as the diffusion of innovation prompting and supporting the ecosystem development.

Diffusion theory supports much of the work of business and industry clusters, and ultimately ecosystems. Early work conducted by scholars from the field of rural sociology traces the impact of county agricultural agents as a means of advancing the diffusion of agricultural innovations (Butler, Chapter 5 in this volume). This line of work expanded to address questions of how certain parts of the United States became home to specific types of business clusters and to the consideration of the role of the community in enhancing cluster development. The first part of the ecosystem creation process was thus the link between individual business creation and regional organizations with their accompanying resources leading to cluster formation.

Bell et al. (2009) provide a useful overview of this cluster approach, starting with Marshall's classic approach to industrial districts (1920). 'Because knowledge becomes more specialized over time, cluster-specific divisions of labor and institutional configurations allow distinctive approaches to problem solving, learning, and knowledge creation to emerge' (Bathelt and Taylor 2002 cited in Bell et al. 2009, 624). This knowledge exchange approach is also emphasized in the recent work of Arikan (2009), who looks at how knowledge creation is enhanced within regional clusters.

The relationship between regional clusters and ecosystems can be taken even further because, while the cluster approach is focused on firms, the interorganizational relationships that lead to collective efficiencies point to a systematic approach, especially when those efficiencies are defined as 'improved access to knowledge and other intangible resources' (Bell et al. 2009, 623). This leads to the acceptance of Porter's grounding definition of clusters as 'a geographically proximate group of interconnected companies and associated institutions' (Porter 2000, 254). Our interest in this book is the role of the university as one of those associated institutions, and the potential of the university to be a catalyst for stimulating the creation of an entrepreneurship ecosystem.

While the original concept of ecosystem stems from the natural sciences, the overarching theoretical framework we use draws from the business ecosystem work of Moore, placing the ecosystem concept as 'an economic community supported by a foundation of interacting organizations and individuals' (Moore 1993). Our framework also links the entrepreneurship ecosystem with concepts like the technopolis, defined as an innovative and research-intensive small and medium-sized enterprise (SME) cluster (Fayolle and Byrne, Chapter 3 in this volume), the innovation value chain defined as idea generation, conversion and diffusion (Hansen and Birkinshaw 2007), and the technopolis defined as 'emphasizing interlocking relationships between academic, business and government' (Scott and Sunder 1998, 8). According to each definition, the characteristics of regional entrepreneurial activity include active engagement (Fayolle and Byrne, Chapter 3 in this volume), the diffusion of entrepreneurial mindsets and skills (Allen and Lieberman, Chapter 4 in this volume) and a systematic approach to collaborative activities throughout the region (Kozmetsky 1993). The emphasis thus lies on the regional dimensions of entrepreneurship, paying particular attention to the influence of regional attributes, and exploring the interdependent relationships between regional environment and entrepreneurial activities and outcomes (Sternberg 2009).

As a refinement of the ecosystem approach, we draw from Aulet's definition of the ecosystem in which he describes the relevant dimensions as individuals, organizations and resources, specifically including government, demand, invention, funding, infrastructure, entrepreneurs and culture (Aulet 2008). This specificity helps us consider the inputs and outcomes of all the ecosystems described in this volume. Every one of these approaches is built on the assumption that a rich set of resources is needed that is often richer in variety than in money.

It may also be useful to consider the scale of ecosystems and to explore commonalities across ecosystems as they expand from the smallest context into progressively larger contexts. The progression might begin with an entrepreneurial venture that is itself an ecosystem, which operates in one element of a U-BEE (for example an incubator). The incubator is part of the overall U-BEE, which in turn operates in a regional cluster. In some cases this nested effect may continue to expand to a national or even global level.

This hierarchy of organizations embodies the concept of fractals; that is, at each level (or scale), the ecosystem reflects the same key success factors. For example the entrepreneurial venture – whether greenfield or corporate – clearly reflects the same or similar success factors attributed to a U-BEE in our concluding chapter. Ventures are indeed building blocks of resources, including the social capital that must connect to other resources and capabilities (Brush et al. 2001). In response to uncertainty, the venture must therefore be a learning organization (requiring teaching by mentors, advisers and more experienced entrepreneurial leaders, as well as research to resolve uncertainties) and must aggressively engage in outreach to access expertise and resources that do not reside in the venture (Rice et al. 2008; Parrish forthcoming). In the same way, some of the elements inside of a U-BEE can also be viewed as entrepreneurship ecosystems in their own right (Rice and Habbershon 2006). For example an incubator (whether operating in a corporate, university or regional economic development context) is itself an entrepreneurship ecosystem (Rice and Habbershon 2006; Rice 1996). This brings us to the consideration of the academic institution, with its capacity to understand, develop and promote entrepreneurial innovation at all levels and in all relationships (Cohen et al. 2005; Fetters et al. 2008). Finally the U-BEE may be among a set of entrepreneurship ecosystems that, when linked together, create a meta-entrepreneurship ecosystem operating at the regional, and in some cases national and global, level.

To return to the chapters in this volume, key aspects of the ecosystem include the alignment of institutional objectives, access to university and other regional resources, coordination of research initiatives, and the participation of the business community and local government at a variety of levels (but starting locally).

OVERVIEW OF SCHOOLS

Our book is divided into two sections. The first three case studies, Babson, EM Lyon and USC, focus on the new venture creation aspects of an entrepreneurship ecosystem. The second three, The University of Texas at Austin, Technológico de Monterrey and NUS, are more focused on technology transfer and commercialization-oriented ecosystems.

Babson College

Babson is a small, private college established as a business institute in 1919 by an entrepreneur, Roger Babson, to teach young men the fundamentals of business. The school has evolved over the years into a co-educational provider of undergraduate and graduate degrees with a specialty in business and an emphasis on entrepreneurship that shapes the school's academic approach in every program. The entrepreneurship ecosystem starting point for Babson was a for-credit course, followed relatively quickly by three flagship programs: the Academy of Distinguished Entrepreneurs (1978), the Babson College Entrepreneurship Research Conference (1980) and the Symposium of Entrepreneurship Educators (1984). Over time, integration of entrepreneurship into the core curriculum, a proliferation of electives and specializations, and innovation and pedagogy established a robust learning environment. Since the turn of the century, Babson has engaged in a dramatic increase in global research programs and globalization with respect to partnership.

EM Lyon Business School

EM Lyon Business School holds a unique position as a *grande école* established by the regional business community, namely the silk industry, and it continues to receive support from the local Chamber of Commerce. However EM Lyon Business School also faces challenges because of the nature of the French educational system, constraining regulation, and less than positive social attitudes toward entrepreneurship. EM Lyon Business School's U-BEE has emerged since the mid-1980s into an engaged extended community with the shared objective of diffusing an entrepreneurial mindset. The ecosystem is built on strategy, institutional infrastructure, teaching and learning, outreach initiatives, development and resources. EM Lyon Business School in 2010 has approximately 2700 degree-seeking students and 93 permanent professors. The school uses an integrated approach that instills entrepreneurship in all undergraduate, graduate and postgraduate programs and includes a PhD program in entrepreneurship launched in 2007. One research center is dedicated to entrepreneurship, focusing on different aspects of creation and growth. EM Lyon has a newly revitalized incubator, which is considered the heart of its entrepreneurial activity, and it uses an online social network as an entrepreneurial hub. The school is strongly linked to external partners including practitioners, academics and policy makers on a local and international level.

University of Southern California (USC)

USC is a large private university located in an urban and diverse area of Los Angeles. The school is a top research university with more than 33 000 students and 3200 full-time faculty members. The area has a number of developed technology clusters and an educated workforce. The entrepreneurship ecosystem at USC started as a multistage, organic process in the early 1960s with a focus on helping students understand the mindset and skills required to launch new businesses. The curriculum for both graduates and undergraduates is delivered through an applied approach and offers an emphasis for graduate students, a minor for undergraduates, and a Certificate in Technology Commercialization, largely pursued by master's degree students and PhD-level researchers in medicine, the sciences, business and engineering. The U-BEE developed over time via the launch of several campus organizations that act as nodes of activities, each one focused on different aspects of entrepreneurial development and technology commercialization. The research mission of the USC ecosystem is organized through the Lloyd Greif Center for Entrepreneurial Studies and targets the development, support and dissemination of leading-edge interdisciplinary scholarship through campus seminars, research conferences and programs to support visiting researchers.

The University of Texas at Austin, IC^2

The University of Texas at Austin is the flagship campus of the state higher educational system. Located in the capital of Texas, the school has

50000 students and 21000 faculty and staff. The heart of the U-BEE at The University of Texas at Austin is the multidisciplinary IC^2 Institute. The launch of the U-BEE was explicitly grounded on a systematic research model based upon diffusion of innovation to transform a region. The original stakeholders were considered to be the university, national scientific laboratories, wealthy Texas families, government and industry. The model focused on new types of linkages among the stakeholders, as well as innovative tools designed to foster collaborative competition. The system grew to include three primary institutional alliances between organizations created by IC^2: the Austin Technology Incubator, the Capital Network and the Texas Technology Incubator. This Austin model is currently being tested in numerous countries around the world with new experiments and alliances added on a regular basis.

Technológico de Monterrey

Technológico de Monterrey is one of the leaders in an organized plan to make Mexico more globally competitive. As part of this effort, federal and state governments are emphasizing high-value activities and sustainability as a long-term strategy, keeping the focus on knowledge-based development through entrepreneurship policy. Technológico de Monterrey is a private university system comprising 33 campuses throughout Mexico; a virtual university; 12 liaison offices in America, Europe and Asia; 106 business incubators and 11 technology parks. The school in 2010 has 100400 students and 8223 faculty members (full- and part-time). The school is committed to five strategic principles for the development of an innovation ecosystem: (1) foster sustainable regional development; (2) capitalize on knowledge for the benefit of society; (3) develop innovation-provoking environments; (4) provide faculty and students the experience of technology transfer, technology commercialization and enterprising/ business incubation; and (5) consolidate Technológico de Monterrey as the academic, scientific and entrepreneurial ally. The ultimate objective is to create an ecosystem that promotes the transfer of knowledge while recognizing and functioning in a way that acknowledges vast economic, political and social differences in the geographic regions that the school supports.

National University of Singapore (NUS)

The entrepreneurial ecosystem of NUS is notable for its location in a relatively small city-state, one that has a strong impetus toward moving to an innovation-driven economy by way of enhancing the entrepreneurial mindset of university graduates. The Singapore government has identified the relatively underdeveloped technology commercialization section of the ecosystem as an impediment in its pursuit of a more robust, innovation-driven economy and has solicited the expertise of NUS in changing Singaporean education to support this economic goal. NUS is not only the oldest and largest public university in Singapore, but it is also the only academic institution there to have achieved the highest research designation from the Carnegie Classification. NUS has over 30 000 students and approximately 2100 faculty members. The hub of the U-BEE is NUS Enterprise, an organization created for just this purpose and intentionally positioned to report to the president of NUS in order to support the development of an integrated entrepreneurship approach. NUS Enterprise operates through five centers, allowing coordination across activities including experiential education, support services, technology licensing, overseas internships, continuing education and the university press. The core goals include embedding experiential entrepreneurial learning into the NUS educational approach and enhancing innovation and commercialization impacts.

OBJECTIVES

There are four primary goals for this book. The first is that it will serve as a resource for academic institutions around the world as they work on developing high-impact entrepreneurship ecosystems. Secondly, we hope it will contribute to building a community of interest among faculty and administrative leaders at universities with highly evolved entrepreneurial ecosystems. The third goal is that this book be a resource for teachers and practitioners as they consider how they use and teach about resources for entrepreneurship. And fourth, we hope to help public policy makers (and funders) understand the significance, complexity, resources needs and contributions of a well-functioning entrepreneurship ecosystem. We see entrepreneurship as a powerful and growing force for addressing global challenges, and U-BEEs as important contributors to the meta-entrepreneurship ecosystem that is developing and supporting entrepreneurs and their ventures around the world.

REFERENCES

Arikan, A.T. (2009), 'Interfirm knowledge exchanges and the knowledge creation capability of clusters', *Academy of Management Review*, **34** (4): 658–76.

Aulet, W. (2008), 'How to build a successful innovation ecosystem: educate, network, and celebrate', *Xconomy.com*, 14 October.

Bathelt, H. and M. Taylor (2002), 'Clusters, power and place: inequality and local growth in time space', *Geografiska Annaler, Series B. Human Geography*, **84** (2), Special Issue: 'Beyond "Happy Communities" in Economic Geography': 93–109.

Bell, S.J., P. Tracey and J.B. Heide (2009), 'The organization of regional clusters', *Academy of Management Review*, **34** (4): 623–42.

Brush, C.G., P.G. Greene and M.M. Hart (2001), 'From initial idea to unique advantage: the entrepreneurial challenge of constructing a resource base', *Academy of Management Executive*, **15** (1): 64–78.

Butler, John Sibley (1991), *Entrepreneurship and Self-Help among Black Americans: A Reconsideration of Race and Economics*, New York: SUNY Press.

Cohen, A.R., M. Fetters and F. Fleischmann (2005), 'Major change at Babson College: curricular and administrative, planned and otherwise', *Advances in Developing Human Resources*, **7** (1): 324–37.

Fetters, Michael, T. Duby and W. Lawler (2008), 'Integration and technology: Innovations that demand faculty development', in *Proceedings of BTC 2008: Teaching Conference for Management Educators*, Wellesley, MA, 11–14 June, pp. 771–4.

Greene, Patricia and John Butler (1996), 'The minority community as a natural business incubator', *Journal of Business Research*, **36**: 51–8.

Hansen, M.T. and J. Birkinshaw (2007), 'The innovation value chain', *Harvard Business Review,* Reprint R0706.

Kozmetsky, George (1993), 'Breaking the mold: reinventing business through community collaboration', Paper presented to the MIT Enterprise Forum, Cambridge, MA 23 October.

Marshall, Alfred (1920), *Principles of Economics*, London: Macmillan.

Moore, James F. (1993), 'Predators and prey: a new ecology of competition', *Harvard Business Review*, May–June: 75–86.

Neck, H.M., B.D. Cohen and A. Corbett (1999), 'A genealogy and taxonomy of high-technology new venture creation within an entrepreneurial system', in P. Reynolds, W.D. Bygrave, K.G. Shaver, C.M. Mason and S. Manigart (eds), *Frontiers of Entrepreneurship Research*, Babson Park, MA: Babson College, pp. 541–55.

Parrish, B.D. (forthcoming), 'Sustainability-driven entrepreneurship: principles of organization design', *Journal of Business Venturing*, doi: 10.1016/j. jbusvent.2009.05.005.

Porter, M. (2000), 'Location, clusters and economic strategy', in G.L. Clark, M. Feldman and M. Gertler (eds), *The Oxford Handbook of Economic Geography*, Oxford: Oxford University Press, pp. 253–74.

Rice, Mark P. (1996), 'Virtuality and uncertainty in the domain of discontinuous innovation', in *Proceedings of International Conference on Engineering and Technology Management (IEEE)*, Vancouver, BC, 18–20 August, pp. 528–32.

Rice, Mark P. and T. Habbershon (2006), 'The Place of Entrepreneurship', in Mark Rice and T.G. Habberson (eds), *Entrepreneurship: The Engine of Growth*, Vol. 3, Westport CT: Greenwood Publishing Group, pp. ix–xxv.

Rice, Mark, G.C. O'Connor and R. Pierantozzi (2008), 'Implementing a learning plan to counter project uncertainty', *Sloan Management Review*, Winter: 54–62.

Scott, Bruce R. and Srinivas Sunder (1998), 'Austin, Texas: building a high-tech economy', Harvard Business School, case number 9-799-038, 8, Cambridge, MA: President and Fellows of Harvard College.

Spilling, O. (1996), 'The entrepreneurial system: on entrepreneurship in the context of a mega-event', *Journal of Business Research*, **36** (1): 91–103.

Sternberg, R. (2009), 'Regional dimensions of entrepreneurship', *Foundations and Trends in Entrepreneurship*, **5** (4): 211–340.

Stinchcombe, A.L. (1965), 'Social structure and organizations', in J.G. March (ed.), *Handbook of Organizations,* Chicago, IL: Rand McNally, pp. 142–93.

Zacharakis, A.L., D.A. Shepherd and J.E. Coombs (2003), 'The development of venture-capital backed internet companies: an ecosystem perspective', *Journal of Business Venturing*, **18**: 217–31.

PART I

Entrepreneurship Ecosystems:
Opportunity-Driven Business Development

2. Babson College

Michael L. Fetters, Patricia G. Greene and Mark P. Rice

INTRODUCTION

In 2010, the current state of Babson's entrepreneurship ecosystem is the result of more than 30 years of intentional design and development in creating a unique community that defines the entrepreneurial approach for higher education. If we start from the premise of the business ecosystem as 'an economic community supported by a foundation of interacting organizations and individuals – the organisms of the business world' (Moore 1993), we can then narrow that definition and be more specific about an entrepreneurial ecosystem as an economic community focused on the development of new and growing companies. At Babson that ecosystem has been deliberately expanded along two significant vectors. Entrepreneurial mindset, the initial major expansion vector, is exemplified by creating and embracing change and ambiguity, fostering a near obsession with opportunity identification, and acting on opportunities within all college sectors as Babson College pursues its own vision. Second, a broader approach to entrepreneurship now includes entrepreneurial thinking and action in established corporations, women's leadership, family enterprises and not-for-profit organizations.

After a brief introduction to Babson, this chapter will be segmented into three sections. We start with a description of the current state of the entrepreneurship ecosystem at Babson; continue with a review of the entrepreneurship ecosystem development discussed around a timeline using the dimensions of teaching, research and outreach; and conclude with a summary of lessons learned and recommendations for schools intent on creating or improving their campus entrepreneurship ecosystem.

William Aulet (2008) provides a systems view of an innovation ecosystem that sets forth useful dimensions that might describe the Babson entrepreneurship ecosystem. Aulet posits that government, demand, invention, funding, infrastructure, entrepreneurs and culture are the primary necessities for the ecosystem. In this chapter we will collapse and adapt these categories and focus primarily on ecosystem governance, ecosystem invention/innovation, ecosystem infrastructure and ecosystem culture.

BABSON COLLEGE: AN INTRODUCTION

Unlike any other academic institution, Babson's history mirrors the history of an entrepreneurial ecosystem. Like many, if not most, private colleges, Babson was founded by an entrepreneur. Roger Babson, successful not only as an entrepreneur but also as an educator and philanthropist, founded Babson in 1919 as an institution specializing in business education. From its launch Babson was intended to provide a practical and explicitly ethical training for young men who wanted to become business executives. In the early days of the school, most students were groomed to return home and work with their fathers in family-owned businesses. Because Babson believed experience was an essential component of a business education, he designed a curriculum that included both classroom study and practical applications. From the start this curriculum was reinforced by group projects, class presentations and meetings with business executives. The students were required to dress in business attire and punch in on a time clock. Their academic work was supported by a secretarial pool so they 'could practice dictating and acting like executives' (Babson College 2007). Daniel Gerber was a member of Babson's first class. After graduation he achieved great success as the founder of Gerber Products, the premier brand of baby food in the United States.

Babson evolved dramatically over its first 75 years. It was called Babson Institute from its launch in 1919 until 1943. During that time Babson offered one- and two-year programs in business administration, and students earned a certificate of completion. The school awarded its first baccalaureate degree in 1947 and its first master's degree in 1953. Women were accepted at Babson beginning in 1968. The next year Babson Institute officially became Babson College (Babson College 2007).

The entrepreneurship ecosystem at Babson College is founded on and supported by the college's vision, mission and values, as well as by the structure and culture of the college as exemplified by the ways in which resources are allocated. While Babson's mission of business education was present at the start, entrepreneurship was increasingly emphasized until 1977, when president Ralph Sorenson made entrepreneurship the explicit focus of the school. This mission was reviewed through an open campus process during the 2007–08 academic year, and entrepreneurship was reaffirmed as the primary driver of the college's strategy:

Mission Statement of Babson College

Babson College educates men and women to be entrepreneurial leaders in a rapidly changing world. We prepare them to identify opportunities and initiate actions that result in genuine accomplishment.

Our innovative curricula challenge students to think creatively and across disciplinary boundaries. We cultivate the willingness to take and manage risk, the ability to energize others toward a goal, and the courage to act responsibly.

Our students appreciate that leadership requires technical knowledge as well as a sophisticated understanding of societies, cultures, institutions, and the self. They welcome the challenge of learning continuously and taking responsibility for their careers. Our students will be key contributors in the world's established enterprises as well as emerging ventures.

At Babson, we collaborate across disciplines and functions to create knowledge and apply integrative solutions to complex problems. We reach across institutional and geographic boundaries to forge relationships with individuals and organizations who share our commitment to excellence and innovation. (www.babson.edu/about/mission)

The emphasis on 'entrepreneurial leaders' in this mission statement is explicit and strategic, but so are other key aspects of the entrepreneurship phenomenon, including opportunities, change, initiative, excellence and a sense of responsibility. Babson also recognizes that its educational philosophy is not limited to the business disciplines. By including the need for a 'sophisticated understanding of societies, cultures, institutions, and the self', Babson acknowledges that a general or liberal arts education is a foundation for entrepreneurial leaders.

ENTREPRENEURSHIP AT BABSON COLLEGE: CURRENT STATE

Ecosystem Governance

Entrepreneurship is encoded in the DNA of Babson. Given that entrepreneurship underlies the mission of the college, the overall responsibility for creating, enhancing and sustaining the entrepreneurship ecosystem is shared by the president, provost and executive leadership team. Babson's governance structure also includes the deans of the three schools: graduate, undergraduate and executive education. The expectations for Babson's leadership team include developing and executing strategies for advancing and promoting entrepreneurship both inside and outside the Babson community. Thus an important part of entrepreneurship ecosystem management is the care and management of the entire system by the executive administration of the college.

While oversight and support by the executive leadership team are necessary to manage the ecosystem, however, they are not sufficient. Others are needed to carry out the design, management and promotion of the ecosystem at Babson. This level of leadership is primarily the responsibility of the chair of the Entrepreneurship Division and the director of the Arthur M. Blank Center for Entrepreneurship. The Babson faculty is divided into ten academic divisions. Given the integrative nature of Babson's curriculum, the primary responsibility of each division chair is to recruit and develop faculty, and secondarily to work with program deans and curriculum review committees to oversee curriculum and program design and their delivery. At Babson this means creating a portfolio of both academic and practice-based faculty, full- and part-time, who can teach, perform research and participate in community building. With respect to teaching, the Entrepreneurship Division chair ensures that entrepreneurship receives appropriate coverage in the undergraduate program, four MBA programs, two MS programs and the Babson executive education program that is delivered in numerous countries around the world.

The chair of the Entrepreneurship Division currently works with more than 40 entrepreneurship faculty members, including ten tenure-track faculty members, 22 adjunct entrepreneurs, a staff of 12 and a changing group of visiting faculty, research associates and student assistants. In addition, eight faculty members from other academic areas have joint appointments or close affiliations with the Entrepreneurship Division. While part of Babson's mission is to be a teaching-first institution, every faculty member is required to be intellectually active. Building strong connections among teaching, research and outreach, each element feeding the other, is explicitly promoted by the division chair. Babson faculty members are encouraged and supported for excellence in teaching, which is considered a threshold competency for tenure, rather than one of several skills that can be traded off. Because Babson is a leader in its field, much of the classroom material has been and continues to be developed by Babson faculty. The primary methods of research at Babson are applied work that targets an audience of entrepreneurs and entrepreneurial leaders, academic research that targets entrepreneurship faculty, and pedagogical research that also targets entrepreneurship faculty. An important role of the chair of the Entrepreneurship Division is to create a group of researchers who address these three categories.

It is significant for the ecosystem approach that the division chair is also a member of the Chairs and Deans Committee chaired by the Babson provost. This committee is where Babson academic strategy is developed, and where entrepreneurship across campus and beyond any single academic division can be discussed. Decisions about the undergraduate and graduate curriculum are also made at these committee meetings.

The second key person in the management of the Babson entrepreneurship ecosystem is the director of the Arthur M. Blank Center for Entrepreneurship. The director is responsible for entrepreneurship outreach on and off the Babson campus, and is particularly active in managing relationships related to entrepreneurial activities. On campus this means overseeing student competitions such as rocket pitches (rapid presentations of business ideas), business plans and incubator spaces; student selection for E-Tower, the dormitory space for entrepreneurship majors; on-campus speakers, and so on. Off campus, the director oversees programs such as the Global Entrepreneurship Monitor (GEM research project), the Babson College Entrepreneurship Research Conference (BCERC), the Symposium for Entrepreneurship Educators (SEE), and the Successful Transgenerational Entrepreneurship Practices (STEP) project, in addition to working with the college's leadership team to host Babson's Academy of Distinguished Entrepreneurs. An important organizational aspect of these initiatives is that they involve separate units that work together but at the same time compete for resources.

This structure supports the entrepreneurial attitude at Babson: Babson's organizational structure is designed to reinforce entrepreneurial academic activity in addition to teaching entrepreneurship. The director works closely with the division chair, but the focus is on programs that are not directly part of the academic curriculum. Their leadership positions are complementary. During the early days of the evolution of the entrepreneurship ecosystem at Babson, one person handled both sets of responsibilities. Operations were limited in scope, resources were scarce and one person could direct both academic tasks and outreach to coordinate the launch and growth of the ecosystem on multiple fronts. But as the field of academic entrepreneurship has grown and the creation of entrepreneurs has become more important to local and national economies, these responsibilities needed to be split in two. Although coordination between the two positions is essential, each one is able to focus on the unique aspects of the job.

Ecosystem Invention/Innovation

Curriculum design

As part of its focus on entrepreneurship, Babson has diligently worked on curricular innovation to achieve its mission of entrepreneurial leadership in a changing global environment. Babson offered its first entrepreneurship course in 1968 and has remained committed to entrepreneurship education since then by launching and supporting a multifaceted approach to curriculum development.

Undergraduate core curriculum   Babson's undergraduate curriculum uses an integrated approach to organize the development of competencies, the understanding of key disciplines and an immersion in the arts and sciences on three levels (foundation, intermediate and advanced) that intersect during the four years of the program. This approach was designed, and continues to be refined, to provide a developmental and holistic approach to learning.

A Babson undergraduate education starts with an interdisciplinary year-long course required of all first-year students: Foundations of Management and Entrepreneurship (FME). Teams of 30 students study an overview of management theory while creating and running a business. The pedagogical technique of organizing students into large teams offers opportunities for students to learn to lead in an entrepreneurial application of most business disciplines. This course also teaches the social entrepreneurship philosophy of doing good while doing well. One leader on each student team plans and coordinates the required community service activities of all team members while the business is being designed and launched. The students liquidate their businesses at the end of their first academic year and compete to see which business donates the most money to their designated community-service organization.

Other freshman-year classes emphasize the development of analytical and cognitive skills, oral and written communication, and ethical decision making through courses offered by both business and liberal arts faculty. The subsequent intermediate and advanced programs allow for increasingly sophisticated interdisciplinary approaches to student development that stress confidence, independence and creativity.

Graduate core curriculum   The required core component of the two-year MBA is designed around the entrepreneurial approach. The program is organized into four integrated modules that follow the life cycle of an entrepreneurial business: Creative Management in Dynamic Organizations, Assessing Business Opportunities, Designing the Delivery System, and Growing Businesses in a Changing Global Environment. The entrepreneurial learning stream is embedded in these four modules. This same approach, modified when appropriate, was used to develop the required coursework in the one-year and blended fast-track MBA programs. The core requirements of the evening MBA have recently been expanded to include a required course entitled Developing Entrepreneurial Opportunities.

Babson has three specialized master's degree programs developed in conjunction with strategic partners. There are two MS degrees in technology entrepreneurship. The first was developed with Babson's sister school, the Franklin W. Olin College of Engineering. It allows an engineering undergraduate student to begin taking master's-level core courses and entrepreneurship elective courses while still completing the requirements for an Olin undergraduate engineering degree. In this accelerated mode, a student can complete both degrees in five years or less. The second MS in Technological Entrepreneurship is a dual degree program offered in collaboration with Tecnológico de Monterrey in Mexico. Its primary purpose is to allow engineering students at Tecnológico de Monterrey to continue their education. Students take two semesters of general business and entrepreneurship courses at Tecnológico de Monterrey while developing their business ideas, and they end the program with a third and final semester of advanced entrepreneurship courses at Babson. The program was co-designed and is co-delivered by Babson and Tecnológico de Monterrey faculty. The third and most recent specialized program is the Tri-Continent MS in Global Entrepreneurship given in partnership with EM Lyon, France, and Zhejiang University, China. In this program, 25 students from each school study and work together on each campus over the course of a year.

Entrepreneurship electives   The integration of entrepreneurship throughout Babson's undergraduate and graduate core curricula began in the 1990s and has continued as a major goal despite numerous governance changes. Perhaps most striking is the comprehensive nature of the development of entrepreneurship electives, which extend entrepreneurial thinking and action into social organizations, major corporations, family enterprises, technology-focused ventures and women's leadership.

Undergraduate electives   After students are introduced during the FME course to new venture creation and management, they are offered an array of entrepreneurship electives from which to choose. Over 90 percent of Babson undergraduates take at least one entrepreneurship elective. Instead of disciplinary majors, Babson students can design concentrations that provide the flexibility to create individualized learning experiences. Initially the development of electives centered on new venture creation; that is, start-ups with explosive growth potential. Core courses entitled New Venture Creation, Entrepreneurial Finance, and Managing a Growing Business were enhanced by the development of electives in Franchising and in Technology-Based Entrepreneurship, as well as managerial consulting field experiences with entrepreneurs, internship programs with venture capitalists and independent studies focused on business plan development for perceived opportunities. Entrepreneurship electives are also expanding into social, corporate, global and women's entrepreneurship, innovation and family enterprises. Other academic disciplines like marketing and economics have developed entrepreneurship electives such as Product Design and Development, and Entrepreneurial Marketing, which are jointly offered across divisions.

Graduate electives   The graduate programs have essentially the same electives as the undergraduate programs, but they are often delivered in different formats. These include both online and intensive time frame courses, for example 1.5 credit courses delivered over three days. The most important recent addition to the entrepreneurship offerings in the graduate school is the Entrepreneurship Intensity Track (EIT). This competitive program requires that students dedicate half their elective credits to the EIT. Once admitted to the program, students work on a business plan during their second year and present it to a panel of experts at the end of the program. These students graduate with an additional EIT designation.

Teaching materials
Case development began early at Babson and is still critical to Babson's entrepreneurship ecosystem. While the Arthur M. Blank Center serves as the development hub, cases are also written across the rest of the campus. Over 90 percent of the cases used by Babson entrepreneurship faculty are developed at Babson. This statistic is important for several reasons. Using a school's own cases establishes its entrepreneurship brand internally and externally, helping not only the school's curriculum but also the teaching of entrepreneurship at other schools. It also presents an opportunity for the case protagonists to attend classes and join discussions, which enhances the students' learning experience. Developing cases also keeps entrepreneurial alumni (the most common source of cases) better connected to the school and builds a network of alumni entrepreneurs to mentor students, support each other and enhance Babson's outreach programs. Case development activities are also a way for Babson faculty to work together across disciplines. While not limited solely to entrepreneurship, 72 Babson faculty members (approximately half the faculty) have written cases as of December 2009.

Cases also serve as another link between Babson and other partners in the ecosystem. Babson creates an average of 10 to 20 cases per year and as of December 2009 has an inventory of almost 300 cases. Approximately 100 of these cases are used on campus each year. In addition 135 Babson cases are distributed by Harvard Business Publishing, which sells 20 000 copies of these cases to 600 colleges around the world. Babson College and Stanford University are the only schools whose cases are distributed through the Harvard system. Babson also serves as the US home to the European Case Clearing House (ECCH), a non-profit organization committed to advancing the use of case-method learning. ECCH serves as another case distribution system for Babson-generated cases.

The other major initiative by Babson faculty is the development of entrepreneurship textbooks. When the field of entrepreneurship emerged, there were no satisfactory texts for classroom use. Inspired by Jeffrey Timmons' textbook, *New Venture Creation* (Timmons et al. 1977), Babson faculty developed a set of textbooks for this new academic field. *The Portable MBA in Entrepreneurship,* edited by William Bygrave (1993), and an undergraduate textbook, *Entrepreneurship,* by William Bygrave and Andrew Zacharakis (2007), are examples of these efforts, with several others currently under development.

Faculty development programs

One of the strongest components of the Babson entrepreneurship ecosystem is the Symposium for Entrepreneurship Educators, the primary mechanism for faculty development. Known internationally as SEE, it is a weeklong program focused on training faculty and entrepreneurs from a variety of disciplines, industries and levels of experience to become entrepreneurship educators. As of December 2009 2400 educators have been trained at the Babson SEE program, with 508 in 2008. Assuming that 60 percent of these SEE alumni are still teaching, and assuming 40 students per class and one class per year, the Babson SEE alumni are educating approximately 60000 students annually. Besides educating faculty worldwide in the art and science of teaching entrepreneurship, SEE has helped many faculty members and administrators better understand entrepreneurship and related curriculum development while building a global network of expertise.

The original SEE program has grown into a strong link between Babson and several global partners in the ecosystem. SEE programs have been customized and delivered to international institutions with the goals of developing international entrepreneurship faculty, expanding the number of entrepreneurship programs globally and generating funds for future Babson entrepreneurship initiatives. SEE also serves as a testing ground for innovative teaching approaches, ranging from the use of ethnographic methodologies to the development of serious games (games that have an educational, training or public policy purpose).

The SEE program was reconfigured for engineering education as the Symposium for Engineer Entrepreneurship Educators (SEEE). Funded by the National Foundation of Science, this program was developed to promote entrepreneurship education in engineering schools. This program jointly delivered by Babson College and the Franklin W. Olin College of Engineering focused on technology-based entrepreneurship education.

Research

The three major components of entrepreneurship research at Babson are: (1) the Babson College Entrepreneurship Research Conference (BCERC); (2) three global entrepreneurship research studies; and (3) dedicated support for research funds for endowed chair holders, as well as post-doctoral and visiting professors. Each of these initiatives has important implications for the teaching and outreach components of the ecosystem. The true value of the Babson ecosystem is its dedication to a continuous increase in the understanding of entrepreneurship. Babson has endeavored over the years to create new ways to support the field of entrepreneurship as it grows and cross-pollinates.

Founded at Babson in 1981, BCERC is considered the premier entrepreneurship research conference in the world. Two out of every three years, the conference is sponsored jointly by Babson and another US or international school, and every third year it is hosted at Babson (see Box 2.1). BCERC is an unusual conference in that attendance is competitive and intentionally limited in number. Early-stage research is encouraged in order to promote invigorating discussions of emerging and innovative ideas. Conference papers are subjected to rigorous peer review, and accepted papers are published in the annual proceedings, *Frontiers of Entrepreneurship Research*. BCERC is an important outlet for entrepreneurship scholars as well as being a networking opportunity for global researchers of entrepreneurship. It also sponsors a doctoral consortium for promising young entrepreneurship scholars. As of December 2009 668 doctoral students from 43 countries have participated in this program.

Babson is home to the three largest multi-country entrepreneurship research studies in the world: GEM (Global Entrepreneurship Monitor); STEP (Successful Transgenerational Entrepreneurship Practices; and the Diana Project, which focuses on women entrepreneurs and entrepreneurial growth. The research partners for each of these projects across the globe are important components of the ecosystem.

GEM monitors over 57 countries to measure and report their entrepreneurial activity and mindset. Its shared methodology allows for comparisons across regions and countries. The GEM researchers also develop special reports that inform entrepreneurs, academics and policy makers about topics like high-growth entrepreneurship, financing and women's entrepreneurship. GEM's databases are periodically entered into the public domain to encourage and support increased research in these areas.

BOX 2.1   BABSON COLLEGE
ENTREPRENEURSHIP RESEARCH
CONFERENCE

2010	International Institute for Management Development (IMD) and Ecole Polytechnique Fédérale de Lausanne (EPFL), Switzerland
2009	Babson College, USA
2008	University of North Carolina at Chapel Hill, Kenan-Flagler Business School, USA
2007	Instituto de Empresa Business School (IEBS), Spain
2006	Indiana University, Kelley School of Business, USA
2005	Babson College and Kauffman Foundation, USA
2004	University of Strathclyde, Hunter Centre for Entrepreneurship, Scotland
2003	Babson College and Kauffman Foundation, USA
2002	University of Colorado at Boulder, Robert H. and Beverly A. Deming Center for Entrepreneurship, USA
2001	Jönköping University, Jönköping International Business School and Swedish Foundation for Small Business Research, Sweden
2000	Babson College and Kauffman Foundation, USA
1999	University of South Carolina, The Darla Moore School of Business, USA
1998	Universiteit Ghent, DeVlerick School voor Management, Belgium
1997	Babson College and Kauffman Foundation, USA
1996	University of Washington, Program in Entrepreneurship and Innovation, USA
1995	London Business School, UK
1994	Babson College and Kauffman Foundation, USA
1993	University of Houston, Small Business Development Center, USA
1992	INSEAD, European Institute of Business Administration, France
1991	University of Pittsburgh, Joseph M. Katz Graduate School of Business Administration, USA
1990	Babson College, USA
1989	Saint Louis University, Institute of Entrepreneurial Studies, USA

1988	University of Calgary, New Venture Development Faculty of Management, Canada
1987	Pepperdine University, Graziadio School of Business and Management, USA
1986	Babson College, USA
1985	University of Pennsylvania, Wharton Entrepreneurial Center, USA
1984	Georgia Institute of Technology, USA
1981–83	Babson College, USA

The STEP project is a research study conducted by a global consortium of academic institutions whose goal is to generate leading-edge data on entrepreneurship in the context of family businesses. Academics who participate in the STEP project are interested in creating a practical nexus between entrepreneurship theory and family-influenced wealth creation. Their institutions support finding practical ways for families to build their entrepreneurial legacies through growth. STEP operates in four regions of the world: Europe, Latin America, Asia and North America. Each region uses the same model but organizes research collection and dissemination independently.

The Diana Project was launched in 1999 by five researchers at five different institutions. Babson serves as the home base for the project since three of the founders are currently connected to Babson, two on the faculty and one on the board of trustees. The Diana Project was established to raise the awareness and expectations of women business owners about the growth of their firms. The founding premise is that the growth of women's businesses is central to wealth creation, innovation and economic development in every country. The creation of the research consortium by the five project partners coincided with the efforts of other groups around the world to support and advance the growth and development of women-owned businesses. A core belief of the Diana Project is that rigorous research is a powerful tool because findings backed by irrefutable data can change attitudes, opinions and practices. The Diana Project has evolved into a global virtual organization that comprises researchers from 28 countries. These researchers use a variety of methodologies to focus on similar questions about women's entrepreneurship, especially those related to growth and the pursuit of capital. Diana International, the organization which oversees the Diana Project as well as the Diana Research Conferences, holds two conferences, one dedicated to supporting entrepreneurs and policy makers and the other to connecting academics around their research.

One valuable outcome of the research component of the ecosystem is the data from the projects that Babson makes public:

- GEM US data for ten years, including at least 2000 respondents per year;
- GEM global data pre-2007, including at least 100000 respondents per year;
- STEP project data related to family business;
- family business data from the Mass Mutual-funded American Family Business Survey (1995, 1997, 2002; www.babson.edu/eship/step);
- Top 100 Business Women in Massachusetts data from the Center for Women's Leadership (six years of data including more than 1000 respondents per survey). Babson dedicates resources to coordinate each of these projects and is looking for new ways to coordinate across projects as well.

A revealing measure of the importance of entrepreneurship in an academic institution is the number of endowed faculty positions. At Babson there are eight endowed positions out of ten tenure-track entrepreneurship faculty members. Endowed positions attract academic leaders and give leading researchers the time to pursue entrepreneurial research and share their findings. For the same reason, postdoctoral and visiting faculty positions are also available at Babson to support research and innovative teaching. These positions must support or enhance Babson faculty research with the objective of writing joint publications. They also bring in additional research talent on an annual basis.

Outreach

Outreach at Babson includes entrepreneurship co-curricular and extracurricular programs for the school and the surrounding community. These programs draw participants from faculty and staff, the business community, alumni and the student body, or more commonly a mixture of all these groups.

The major outreach events for faculty and staff, like the Babson College Entrepreneurship Research Conference and the multi-site research studies (GEM, STEP and Diana) overlap with teaching and research. They contribute to a vibrant campus entrepreneurship ecosystem by encouraging new ideas based on research and by extending Babson's entrepreneurship reputation. Even more importantly they promote entrepreneurial thinking and action worldwide. They address the increasingly important challenge of stimulating economic and social development around the world through entrepreneurship. The Symposium for Entrepreneurship Educators (SEE), as described previously, is a major outreach program for Babson in the academic and practitioner community. Faculty members from around the world have participated in Babson SEE programs offered in Wellesley, MA, and in countries in South and Central America, Europe and Asia.

Babson's annual Founders' Day, which features the Academy of Distinguished Entrepreneurs (ADE), is a visible and successful part of the outreach portfolio. This tradition began in 1978 when Babson, at the time a small college with a regional reputation, invited Soichiro Honda (Honda), Berry Gordy (Motown Records), Ray Kroc (McDonald's), Roy Little (Textron) and Kenneth Olsen (Digital Equipment Company) to celebrate their entrepreneurial accomplishments on campus. This gathering of renowned business leaders helped convince the Babson community of the viability of an academic entrepreneurship focus while it advanced Babson's reputation for entrepreneurship in the external world. The evolution and importance of the ADE to Babson's entrepreneurship ecosystem will be discussed in more detail in the next section.

Babson requires students to be entrepreneurial in designing their schedules, programs and celebrations. Giving students the authority and responsibility to plan co-curricular and extracurricular activities is critical to the vibrancy of the ecosystem. Student creativity and energy is harnessed to plan and execute an almost constant (and sometimes overwhelming) series of entrepreneurship events. Babson students also apply their entrepreneurial thinking and energy off campus by working with small businesses and not-for-profit organizations as volunteers or as part of their course work. This creates an entrepreneurship buzz on campus that is like oxygen for the ecosystem.

Student events include rocket pitch and business plan competitions plus competitions for incubator space (known as hatcheries) at Babson. Facilities are available for graduate and undergraduate students who have submitted new venture creation plans. Babson has also joined the F.W. Olin College of Engineering to open incubator space on both campuses to joint teams of Olin and Babson students. Students organize, sponsor and run annual hosted speaker series, major symposia and all-day conferences. Another part of the ecosystem is the E-Tower, a collection of dorm spaces dedicated to undergraduate entrepreneurship students. Acceptance into this residential space is competitive because E-Tower programs include guest speakers, panels of advisors, frequent dinners with faculty and campus-wide programs organized by the E-Tower residents.

Babson alumni are another major component of the ecosystem. They serve as resources for case writing, campus panels, speakers at receptions and admissions tours, affinity groups based on entrepreneurship, investors and board members for student-generated businesses. They also function as a lively advisory network for the Babson community. Alumni remain active in the ecosystem by sponsoring entrepreneurship internships, hiring graduates and giving feedback on ideas, opportunities and business plans. They also play a critical role in grounding the curriculum in the real world by connecting students and faculty to entrepreneurial practice. An alumni information systems network invites Babson alumni to judge the first round of the student business plan competitions.

Babson's strategy in working with professional organizations and foundations focused on entrepreneurship is to expand the field of entrepreneurship and enhance Babson's reputation in this space. The Kauffman Foundation, the Association to Advance Collegiate Schools of Business (AACSB), the Academy of Management (AOM), the United States Association for Small Business and Entrepreneurship (USASBE) and the European Foundation for Management Development (EFMD) have been at the center of this strategy. The academic council (provost and school deans) and the entrepreneurship faculty have developed strategies and assignments to establish a significant Babson presence is these organizations.

Ecosystem Infrastructure

Babson's infrastructure consolidates progress in its entrepreneurship ecosystem development and enhances the growth of the ecosystem by infusing entrepreneurship throughout the campus. While infrastructure clearly involves space, administrative positions and communication systems are also critical components. For example in the early 2000s the entrepreneurship group, in conjunction with alumni relations and IT, created a networking system that allows Babson alumni to be 'judges at a distance' in the early rounds of student business plan competitions. This infrastructure meets the goal of keeping alumni connected while creating a sense of community among students.

The importance of space to the ecosystem cannot be overemphasized. In businesses people have traditionally aspired to a corner office. On campuses, space symbolizes permanence, prestige and strategic importance, all of which increase campus mindshare and support ecosystem development. Often a visitor's first impression of Babson is a particular building, office or meeting room. A building can draw attention to a strategically important initiative or segment of the organization. There was already a fairly small entrepreneurship center at Babson before Arthur M. Blank, a Babson alumnus and co-founder of Home Depot, endowed a new building that quickly became the focal point for all entrepreneurial activities at Babson.

The Arthur M. Blank Center, which opened in 1998, is the gathering place for visiting professors, major research studies, community angel investing groups and others who might not have come to Babson previously.

Over the years an administrative staff has taken shape at Babson that supports entrepreneurship champions on campus. Program directors, research directors, marketing specialists, development officers and student advisors are all critical to the successful development of the entrepreneurship ecosystem.

Babson's entrepreneurship champions work closely with both campus information technology (IT) and development to create, maintain and expand communication systems. This segment of the infrastructure is increasingly important as the ecosystem grows and the stimulants of this growth are more varied and widespread.

Ecosystem Culture

While culture has been defined from many perspectives, for the purposes of this chapter it is defined as the values, norms and climate of an organization (Schein 1983; Katz and Kahn 1978) that authentically represent the organization's identity. The Babson mission, as described earlier, articulates its entrepreneurial dimensions. It guides decision-making and steers resource allocation toward the institutional vision of being the globally recognized leader in entrepreneurial management education. Babson's goal is to be known for thought leadership that advances management practice and theory, and to be respected as an academic community of committed, diverse and highly qualified students, faculty and staff. Over time the innovative management programs have been recognized for excellence, and Babson graduates are demonstrating entrepreneurial and ethical leadership in communities around the world.

A coordinated approach to achieving these goals is supported by the Babson values of integrity, diversity, innovation and collaboration. While several of these values can be found on most organizational lists, and each one is necessary in entrepreneurship education, innovation and collaboration are less often cited as core values, and therefore they better differentiate Babson in the marketplace. Babson's definition of innovation is also significant: 'We have a long-standing commitment to an institutional culture that fosters creativity, risk-taking, continuous improvement, leadership, and an entrepreneurial spirit. We encourage people to take the initiative and make a difference' (www.babson.edu/about/values). This dedication to innovation is evident in the pursuit of new programs, content and pedagogy, and it encompasses permission to fail, a message that has encouraged academic experimentation.

Collaboration is one of the core values of Babson College, as defined in the following statement:

> Our commitment to cross-disciplinary collaboration and to working closely with students defines the practices of the faculty, administration, staff and those who work on the campus of Babson College. Together with our alumni, and with our external partners, we create a learning and working experience that is greater than the sum of its parts.

Creating an institutional mandate to work across boundaries makes a significant difference in the battle against the organizational tendency to create and defend silos.

Babson's culture also opposes the tendency for faculty to define themselves according to their allegiance to an academic discipline rather than to the school. Visitors have often observed that at Babson, faculty and staff have a strong attachment to the school that transcends other allegiances and leads to more integrated decision making. This overarching loyalty becomes another organizational resource for the ecosystem.

Babson is considered a fast-paced work environment. The college's values mean that there are often many projects in the pipeline, under development, being delivered or being reviewed. Reflecting the values of inclusion and integration, many voices are sought and heard as projects take shape. Making sense of these myriad voices is a challenge that cuts across many dimensions of the entrepreneurial ecosystem. Perhaps the most problematic part of this challenge is to define what and who is included under the label of entrepreneurship and what this definition means to the various stakeholders. The definition is particularly important in relation to the distribution of resources and to overall perceptions of equity.

THE EVOLUTION OF BABSON'S ENTREPRENEURSHIP ECOSYSTEM

'A business ecosystem, like its biological counterpart, gradually moves from a random collection of elements to a more structured community'. Business ecosystems are often described in stages: birth, expansion, leadership and self-renewal (Moore 1993). The entrepreneurial ecosystem at Babson has evolved according to this sequence. This does not mean that there have been no incremental changes in between. But interviews with past presidents, entrepreneurship center directors, chairs of the entrepreneurship division and faculty who were present during the maturation of the ecosystem confirm that certain major events changed the trajectory of entrepreneurship at Babson and perhaps around the world. The

---

BOX 2.2   BABSON COLLEGE ENTREPRENEURSHIP TIMELINE

1977   Babson establishes Academy of Distinguished Entrepreneurs
1978   First Center for Entrepreneurship Studies in the world
1979   Undergraduate program, first entrepreneurship major
1981   Babson College Entrepreneurship Research Conference (BCERC)
1984   First undergraduate business plan competition, Price-Babson Symposium for Entrepreneurship Educators (SEE)
1987   First business plan competition for MBA students
1993   First full-time MBA with entrepreneurship, new venture creation at its core
1996   Diana Project
1998   Babson Business Hatchery opens, Arthur M. Blank Center opens
1999   Babson College Seed Fund, Global Entrepreneurship Monitor (GEM) initiated
2005   STEP
2008   Babson Entrepreneurship Monitor (BEM)

---

timeline in Box 2.2 shows the major events in the development of Babson' ecosystem.

In the mid-1990s during a field trip to Cognac, France, that was part of a Babson graduate course called Doing Business in Europe, Jean Pierre Camus gave an excellent presentation about the Cognac industry. A member of one of only six families that produce Cognac, he began by saying, 'Being an excellent producer of Cognac is easy: your great-great grandfather, great-grandfather, grandfather and father just have to teach you.' This amusing advice is a simplification but it highlights the importance of tradition and heredity in the building of an ecosystem. In the mid-1970s the new president of Babson, Ralph K. Sorenson, was trying to develop a deeper understanding of Babson's heritage and decide how to use it to differentiate Babson from other schools, and thereby create a new educational paradigm. President Sorenson reasoned that Babson, founded in 1919 and located near Boston, the home of world-class universities, could not compete head-to-head with more famous schools. As he studied the history of Babson, he saw that Babson's founder, Roger Babson, had been an entrepreneur and that numerous Babson alumni had started and run successful new ventures. At the same time he learned that a management professor, Jack Hornaday, wanted to teach entrepreneurship from a human behavior perspective. Hornaday was an organizational psychologist interested in the characteristics of people who had started their own businesses, and he had recently added a segment on entrepreneurs to one of his courses. Sorenson realized that there was something in Babson's heritage that could be used to build a unique education program.

The major impetus for the ensuing stage of development came from the creation of the Academy of Distinguished Entrepreneurs (ADE), which was itself enhanced by the creation of three courses in entrepreneurship and the funding of an endowed chair in entrepreneurship. ADE was created to celebrate entrepreneurs, people who had launched new ventures and led them through a period of hyper-growth to become immensely successful businesses. When ADE was established in 1978, no other organized celebration of entrepreneurship existed. Connecting Babson with entrepreneurship in this way turned the spotlight on Babson. But because of its regional reputation, Babson needed a partnership with a well-known organization to maximize this attention. The Babson leadership team sold the idea of a partnership to the Forbes family and *Forbes* magazine, which in turn helped convince executives from *Business Week* and the *Wall Street Journal* to serve as judges to select the honorees for the ADE. Along with Babson representatives, the judges developed selection criteria, vetted nominees and partnered in inviting and securing participation of nominees.

At the same time two major academic initiatives were being launched: the development and delivery of three new entrepreneurship courses and the funding of an endowed chair in entrepreneurship. The entrepreneurship courses were Introduction to Entrepreneurship, New Venture Creation and Entrepreneurship Finance. In the Babson tradition, which meshed well with entrepreneurship, the courses were more applied than theoretical, based on cases and experiential learning. All three courses covered how to write business plans, an important topic but redundant for students who were enrolled in them all. Even though this part of the course design was flawed, the outcome was that Babson established an entrepreneurship curriculum beyond a single course, which in turn laid the foundation for an entrepreneurship major.

A complementary initiative was the creation of an endowed chair in entrepreneurship funded by the Babson family in 1979. Endowed chairs are an important currency in academic institutions because the permanence of the endowed position represents the importance of the strategic initiative. When this chair was created, there were few if any endowed chairs in entrepreneurship. Through the symbolism of this chair, President Sorenson communicated to the Babson community his commitment to entrepreneurship and also communicated to the external community that Babson intended to identify itself formally with entrepreneurship. The ADE, the new courses and the endowed chair were the first strategic wave that propelled Babson into the entrepreneurship spotlight and entrepreneurship into the business spotlight.

In the late 1970s and well into the 1990s, the external world, both business and academia, did not particularly value entrepreneurship. But when the United States and then the world discovered entrepreneurship, Babson was ready with teaching materials, research and linkages between academia and the entrepreneurs who were creating new ventures. Probably no one was better positioned or a more dynamic and effective advocate for entrepreneurship than Jeffry Timmons. As the importance of entrepreneurship grew, Timmons embarked on a mission to spread entrepreneurship around the world. His seminal textbook, *New Venture Creation: A Guide to Small Business Development* (Timmons et al. 1977), which appeared in six subsequent editions, his creation of the Symposium for Entrepreneurship Educators, and his work with the Kauffman Foundation and Ernst & Young are all examples of his entrepreneurship missionary work.

The major forces creating the second wave of development were the formation of the Center for Entrepreneurship at Babson, the creation of a major in Entrepreneurship for undergraduates and the Babson College Entrepreneurship Research Conference (BCERC). The establishment of the Center for Entrepreneurship (the Center) was again a powerful signal to the Babson community of the importance and permanence of entrepreneurship. A top-down approach to entrepreneurship development at Babson had always been a given. As the focus on entrepreneurship gained momentum, the Babson community received a steady flow of evidence from the academic leadership team that supported the importance of entrepreneurship both as an academic discipline and as a core strategy for Babson. The Center was a catalyst for the creation of permanent champions for entrepreneurship on campus because it gave them a home. It also gave the president evidence to point to when describing Babson's leadership in entrepreneurship, especially during fundraising campaigns. And it provided an infrastructure where individual initiatives could be collected, organized and promoted. This infrastructure was important in allowing the creativity of faculty and students to develop entrepreneurially. New ideas were reviewed by the Center for Entrepreneurship staff, small amounts of funding were provided and administrative support was available to help execute new initiatives.

In other words, at a time when the leadership team was setting the course from the top down, the Center encouraged and supported bottom-up innovation. Babson has always fostered creativity and individual initiative. While this combination may at times produce a rather chaotic campus environment, new ideas and energy also advance Babson's efforts in entrepreneurship. An entrepreneurial culture reinforces the centrality of entrepreneurship as an academic discipline. With the creation of the Center, faculty, staff, students, alumni and friends of the Babson community were invited to be entrepreneurs in developing the field of entrepreneurship.

Although a few entrepreneurship electives had been created by this time, these courses reflected the individual interests of their professors and were largely uncoordinated. The founding director of the Center, William Bygrave, knew that an academic major had to be created to give entrepreneurship stature within the Babson community. Bygrave's survey of current courses showed that they all revolved around business plans. They were good courses but had little logical flow from one to another. He also discovered confusion on campus and within the entrepreneurship faculty about the differences between small business management and entrepreneurship. Bygrave reasoned, and the Babson community agreed, that Babson's brand of entrepreneurship should be based on the creation of new ventures with high growth potential rather than lifestyle ventures or cottage-industry businesses. He initiated three courses – New Venture Creation, Entrepreneurial Finance and Managing a Growing Business – as the core of the entrepreneurship major. Other electives included Franchising, Family Business, and a field-based independent study course. Bygrave also worked with other academic divisions to create joint majors with entrepreneurship, thereby opening the field of entrepreneurship to other academic divisions and expanding the offerings available to entrepreneurship majors.

The third major force that supported Babson's expansion was initiated by Karl Vesper, the first (temporary) holder of the endowed chair in entrepreneurship. Vesper created the Babson College Entrepreneurship Research Conference in 1981 as an invitation-only meeting to discuss and promote early-stage entrepreneurship research. About a decade later, Babson worked with the Center for Entrepreneurial Leadership at the Kauffman Foundation to expand the research conference, to make applications competitive, to create a consortium supporting doctoral candidates doing entrepreneurship research, and to produce a professional publication of the best research papers presented each year at the conference. The conference grew from 35 participants and papers to well over 200 papers presented in 2008, and in the process became the pre-eminent entrepreneurship research conference in the world. Just as the Forbes family accelerated and increased the impact of the ADE, so too did the funding and involvement of the Kauffman Foundation give BCERC greater stability, professionalism, sustainability and an increased impact on the world of academic entrepreneurship.

For Babson, a school with no doctoral programs, this conference was important in establishing its academic credentials. Sponsorship of a major research conference and a highly esteemed annual research publication demonstrated to research-oriented universities that Babson's focus on entrepreneurship included research as well as curriculum development, case writing and connections to the practice of entrepreneurship. At this time Babson also began to develop a strategy of working with organizations such as the AOM and the AACSB to promote the discipline of entrepreneurship, and Babson as a center of entrepreneurship activity. At first this meant that deans, entrepreneurship faculty and the academic vice-president presented papers at academic meetings and worked with foundations interested in entrepreneurship. Eventually this effort evolved into a coordinated strategy executed by Babson administration, the chair of the Entrepreneurship Division, faculty and the director of the Arthur M. Blank Center for Entrepreneurship. They were given responsibilities to work with specific organizations to promote Babson and entrepreneurship. For instance the dean of the graduate school and the academic vice-president focused on AACSB and certain faculty members focused on AOM.

For entrepreneurship as an academic discipline, this was the first major research conference to provide a stimulus and an outlet for research focused on entrepreneurship. It was also a useful networking vehicle that connected researchers, stimulated new research vectors and supported entrepreneurship faculty at other universities. Entrepreneurship faculty support at other universities turned out to be an important benefit of BCERC, so much so that it spawned an idea that triggered the next wave of development, the Symposium for Entrepreneurship Educators.

The Symposium for Entrepreneurship Educators (SEE) was the brainchild of Jeffry Timmons. The objective of SEE was to increase entrepreneurship faculty, curriculum and programs by sharing Babson's curriculum, pedagogy and experience with faculty around the world. The week-long SEE seminar focused on how to teach entrepreneurship, curriculum development, case writing and classroom management. Equally important was the objective of increasing the number of entrepreneurship faculty. Timmons proposed to do this in a uniquely Babson way.

As a business school, especially a business school focused on entrepreneurship, Babson's goal was to teach an applied curriculum supported by research. Students needed to be action-oriented so that they could make an immediate impact in their business careers. While conceptual research is important and accepted at Babson, applied research and teaching (that is, case-based teaching and field-based learning) are the cornerstones of Babson's curriculum and intellectual vitality. Timmons required every professor to bring to SEE an entrepreneur who was willing to teach. The benefits were immediate. New entrepreneurship faculty were created, the entrepreneurs kept classroom discussions grounded in the reality of new venture creation, and the entrepreneurs became an important source of funding for the schools that participated in SEE.

After SEE was off the ground and seemed successful, Timmons and the Babson president at the time, William Dill, secured funding for SEE from the Price Foundation. The benefits of this association were a reputation boost provided by the Price Foundation, resources to expand SEE and give scholarships to faculty from schools that could not support the travel and tuition, and a new Babson trustee named Gloria Appel, who became a devoted supporter of entrepreneurship. As happened with BCERC, external funding proved to be an important component in creating a successful entrepreneurship ecosystem.

Another major initiative at this stage was the formation of the student-led Entrepreneurship Exchange (the Exchange). Although students had been critical to the focus and success of ADE and certainly important in creating enthusiasm for the entrepreneurship curriculum, the Exchange gave students a formal space in the Entrepreneurship Center and the authority, as well as the responsibility, to create and run their own entrepreneurship programs on campus. Sometimes on their own, sometimes partnered with faculty and sometimes partnered with Babson administration, the students were central in establishing the business plan competition, the hatchery space competition, the creation and sponsorship of an annual day-long entrepreneurship event, student hosts for ADE, the creation of a dorm space dedicated to entrepreneurship students (E-Tower) and numerous other activities. The Exchange unleashed the creativity of the students and created a constant buzz around entrepreneurship. The variety of activities augmented Babson's entrepreneurship brand globally with SEE and also escalated student interest in entrepreneurship on campus. In retrospect, SEE was perfectly timed, but the Exchange should have been created earlier in the Babson timeline.

Several factors accelerated Babson's rise to a leadership position in entrepreneurship, but the two main ones were interactions with major organizations outside Babson. The first was a successful effort by the Babson president to lobby the magazine *US News and World Report* to rank specialty schools (that is, schools focused only on one area like art or business) and develop an entrepreneurship ranking. The second was an attempt by the academic leadership to raise Babson's profile in the major organizations influencing entrepreneurship and school rankings. Some of these efforts confirmed previous strategies, like the close relationship with the Kauffman Foundation and the increased presence in AACSB, but others were new, like targeting AOM, the United States Association for Small Business and Entrepreneurship (USASBE) and the National Collegiate Inventors and Innovators Alliance (NIICA). Professor Andrew Zacharakis focused on AOM by joining the research and teaching committees in the entrepreneurship division. He was soon asked to take a leadership position and over a five-year period served as pre-conference chair, conference chair, division president-elect, division president and past president. To target USASBE, Babson, led by Professor Heidi Neck, entered and won a competition about curriculum innovation. Subsequently Professor Neck was elected to the USASBE board and asked to join the Vision 2020 task force, whose mission was to create a strategic direction for the organization.

Babson recognized the importance of professional organizations and accrediting agencies like AACSB and EFMD, while also helping deans, provosts and presidents of colleges and universities gain a better understanding of entrepreneurship education in order to support programmatic growth. Babson administrators helped AACSB found and grow the Entrepreneurship Interest Group, which offers program design and content on a regular basis. Members of the Babson community also helped EFMD by participating in entrepreneurship programs, including hosting educational programs for new deans from around the world.

Four major initiatives in the 1990s were crucial in solidifying Babson's entrepreneurship ecosystem: the revision of Babson's curriculum to include entrepreneurship, the building of the Arthur M. Blank Center for Entrepreneurship, the launch of the Global Entrepreneurship Monitor (GEM) research project, and the extension of entrepreneurship into new domains and locations around the world. Together they confirmed Babson's leadership position in the field of entrepreneurship.

Instilling entrepreneurship into core business courses happened in stages, but these stages were intertwined and therefore better described as they relate to undergraduate, graduate and executive education programs. Although a great deal of the entrepreneurship curriculum development had taken place in the undergraduate program, especially elective courses, the graduate school led the way in infusing entrepreneurship into the core curriculum. A combination of both external and internal factors showed the opportunity and the need to differentiate Babson's MBA program. Guided by the entrepreneurial mission, in the early 1990s a group of faculty and administrators redesigned the core requirements of Babson's two-year MBA program. They organized it into four modules: Creativity and Leadership, Assessing Opportunities, Designing the Delivery Systems, and Growing a Global Business. To remove the constraint of thinking in terms of courses, they designed learning streams (blocks of material shorter than a course and designed to be delivered only when the students needed the information) around these four modules. The guiding principles were entrepreneurial thinking and action, integrative learning and just-in-time presentation of topics. The Entrepreneurship Division faculty also created learning streams that were woven into the four modules. The success of this redesign was extraordinary. Within five years (1993–98) enrollments increased by 60 percent, average GMAT scores, the graduate business school admissions examination required of all graduate school applicants, jumped 75 points and Babson was ranked in the top 50 MBA programs in the United States. The success of this program redesign was also the basis for the most successful fund-raising campaign in Babson's history and provided the impetus to replicate these changes in the undergraduate and executive education programs.

Three major curriculum revisions were undertaken in the undergraduate program. A first-year required course, Foundations of Management and Entrepreneurship (FME), was redesigned around new venture creation. The second revision was to integrate and combine 13 intermediate-level required business courses into three courses taken over three semesters. The integrated courses focused on large companies as well as start-ups. In the new curriculum, students complete their core requirements in the middle of their third year and then proceed to the advanced portion of their coursework, electives. Not surprisingly, over 90 percent of Babson students take at least one elective in entrepreneurship. An Advanced Course in Entrepreneurship (ACE) was created for second-year students who were determined to be entrepreneurs, who had entrepreneurship experience before coming to Babson, who had done well in FME and who wanted to maintain their ongoing entrepreneurial activities.

The result of these revisions is that entrepreneurship is now at the heart of Babson's required business core curriculum. Their positive learning experiences have motivated students to take entrepreneurship electives and to engage in the entrepreneurship ecosystem at Babson. Students who do not necessarily plan to start an entrepreneurial venture are still interested in entrepreneurship, they collaborate on projects, they take pride in Babson's entrepreneurial culture, and they think more innovatively.

Not surprisingly, entrepreneurship and innovation have become crucial in differentiating Babson's executive education offerings. In the mid-1990s the MBA program had recently been redesigned and launched when a European company contacted the director of Babson Executive Education with a request for a program. Babson designed a program to help high-potential mid-level managers enhance their entrepreneurial thinking and activities and thereby stimulate company growth. As this program was rolled out through the company over three years, it became clear that those who had completed it were changing the corporate culture. However they felt they could move even faster if the financial gatekeepers were also more entrepreneurial. So Babson designed another program for the finance staff to teach entrepreneurial thinking and activity. Over the next decade this company continued to be one of Babson's largest clients as the corporate culture changed from a traditional operational focus to becoming entrepreneurial and opportunity-driven. Entrepreneurship is at the core of all Babson learning programs, undergraduate, graduate and executive education.

In 1999 Babson and the London Business School developed the Global Entrepreneurship Monitor (GEM). Led by Professor William Bygrave of Babson and Professor Michael Hay of the London Business School, GEM was designed to measure entrepreneurship activities and attitudes in countries around the world. Today GEM collects and publishes data on 57 countries and influences governmental policies to stimulate entrepreneurship attitudes and activities. Through its yearly reports, this project has been a catalyst for important entrepreneurship research. It has influenced government policies and heightened awareness of the importance of entrepreneurship worldwide. As one example, in response to GEM findings in Great Britain, the government changed the public school curriculum to encourage more creative thinking and entrepreneurial attitudes in British students. These positive results expanded Babson's entrepreneurship brand and reinforced the importance of entrepreneurship in the Babson community, and the additional visibility nourished Babson's entrepreneurship ecosystem. The research competencies provided by GEM also allowed Babson to create and manage another multisite, multipartner global study in family enterprises (the STEP Project) and to serve as one of the hosts of the Diana Project, a global research agenda for women entrepreneurs.

The expansion of the intellectual domain of entrepreneurship from new venture creation into family business, corporations, social ventures and women's leadership began slowly and then picked up speed. The new domains reflected the realization that in a rapidly changing world, entrepreneurial thinking and action were requirements for success in every kind of enterprise, large and small, for-profit and not-for-profit, private and public. Creativity, opportunity recognition and innovation in support of entrepreneurial leadership were as important as the traditional managerial capabilities of cost control and supply chain management that support ongoing operations and maximize short-term results. With this extended definition, more of the Babson community could connect to entrepreneurship and thus enlarge the entrepreneurship ecosystem.

Along with this expansion of the definition of entrepreneurship came an effort to carry Babson's model to other regions of the world. The tools used for this expansion were the Symposium for Entrepreneurship Educators (SEE) and a network of strategic partnerships with international schools interested in entrepreneurship. Three institutes were created that represented Asia, Europe and Latin America. Each one had a faculty director responsible for formulating regional strategy, working with Babson's academic council (the provost's office and deans) to determine future actions and acting as the champion at the respective institutes. The first steps in creating the network were to develop a Babson alumni network in the region, identify and contact regional universities suitable for partnerships, and explore funding sources. The goal of each institute was to create eventually a network of well-known schools focused on entrepreneurship and interested in multidimensional relationships with Babson. Possible dimensions of these relationships are entrepreneurship research, student and faculty exchanges, case development, executive education and joint programs.

As of December 2009 Babson has developed a number of high-quality partnerships in the three regions with a total of 17 schools around the world. The results are new cases, joint executive education and degrees, curriculum sharing and exchanges, new research (STEP was formulated and launched in the three regions with the partner schools) and dual- and tri-degree programs. But perhaps the biggest success has been the expansion of SEE. Since 2004 SEE has been delivered in five Latin American countries, two European countries and two Asian countries (China and Malaysia). All these successes have played a part in ensuring renewal and sustainability for the entrepreneurship ecosystem at Babson.

THE FUTURE

The mission of Babson's newest initiative, the Lewis Institute, is to develop leaders, create new knowledge and grow new enterprises to solve compelling global problems. After three years of planning, in October 2008 the Institute was funded and launched, and will use the skills, knowledge and attitudes of the entrepreneur to create value in the areas of education, health care, communication and infrastructure, economic development, security, sustainability, energy, the environment and the quality of life. Looking to the future, Babson's new president, Leonard Schlesinger, is committed to expanding entrepreneurial thinking and action more comprehensively throughout the activities of the Babson community. Every academic division is currently exploring linkages in terms of both curriculum and research to entrepreneurial thinking and action, in order to increase the force behind Babson's leadership in entrepreneurship and Babson's strategy through the Lewis Institute to harness entrepreneurial thinking and action to address compelling global problems.

KEY SUCCESS FACTORS

New initiatives may begin small, like a pilot project, but they must be able to evolve into a multipronged, sustainable comprehensive program in order to be successful. This is especially true if the development of a comprehensive and robust ecosystem is the goal. It helps to have a tradition of entrepreneurship or at least some successful entrepreneurs among alumni and students. In addition to being founded by an entrepreneur, Babson has produced many entrepreneurial alumni who supported the school's focus on entrepreneurship and provided advice, energy and resources. The success stories of Arthur Blank, co-founder of Home Depot; Craig Benson, co-founder of Cabletron Systems; and Gustavo Cisneros, President and CEO of Organization Diego Cisneros (ODC) underscore the school's reputation and help establish the entrepreneurial culture. Entrepreneurship must be grounded in the school's history, faculty and alumni proponents must be identified, and a logical foundation for pursuing entrepreneurship across campus must be built upon. Uncovering and communicating these stories establishes a culture that supports entrepreneurship.

The president can establish strategic intent and launch an entrepreneurship ecosystem, but a carefully selected implementation team composed of representatives of all community stakeholders must become ardent champions of their product. In other words, it takes a powerful and committed team to sustain the creativity, energy and work necessary to build an entrepreneurship ecosystem. The president must stay involved, communicate goals and raise funds, but one person cannot build the ecosystem. In fact one of the team's challenges is to help the president stay on course when other challenges and opportunities demand attention and energy.

Competencies in entrepreneurship must be developed, secured and sustained. Unless a school succeeds in developing and sustaining a high level of research, teaching and outreach, the ecosystem will be not be sustainable. It is not sufficient to declare the importance of entrepreneurship if there are no people who actually know something about it, as has happened at a number of schools, because there will not be enough entrepreneurship substance to sustain the declaration of entrepreneurship authority. Entrepreneurship builders must be found who are respected teachers and researchers and successful entrepreneurs. Here it might be best to think about constructing a portfolio of talents. A combination of excellent research faculty, dynamic teachers and professors of practice who were successful entrepreneurs is necessary to create the substance of the ecosystem.

The creation of an entrepreneurship ecosystem can occur in waves or stages. Although the sequence of the stages may vary from school to school, every stage needs to be multidimensional and integrated both within and across stages, and it must create energy and synergy on and off campus. Creating programs piecemeal or as one-off initiatives with the promise of more to come undermines the perception of sustainability and comprehensiveness, and it frequently results in an evolutionary process that is too long and insufficiently intensive to maintain stakeholders' attention. Concentration will falter if an institution does not move forward fast with visible projects creating recognizable successes in entrepreneurship internally as well externally.

Major external funding is critical for several reasons. New resources signal the importance of the initiative to the campus; outside funding is a stamp of approval from an external source, which is important for brand building; earmarked resources reassure campus stakeholders that internal funding is not being taken from other initiatives; and foundations frequently extend the impact of campus ecosystems by means of network access, additional funding and promotion of the project in the foundation's literature. It must be emphasized that strategically invested internal funds often make it possible to target and acquire external funds.

When the entrepreneurship ecosystem is looked at as an extended enterprise, establishing external partnerships is essential, especially for smaller schools like Babson. One lesson of entrepreneurship is that if you start alone, you have only your own financial and human resources, intellectual property and social capital. But if you work with partners, you have access to the resources in their ecosystems as well. For Babson, this lesson applies to how we teach, perform research and expand outreach.

Scaling opportunities must be quickly identified and obsessively pursued. Rapid scaling of initiatives changes the trajectory of ecosystem development and creates a virtuous circle of impact, recognition, feedback, improvement and growth. Scaling is necessary to create an ecosystem of substance, which in turn generates the campus-wide enthusiasm that enables the entrepreneurship system to become self-sustaining.

Entrepreneurship ecosystems can be developed in many ways, from a variety of starting points and led by different stakeholders depending on the institution, the educational system and the economic environment in which it operates. This chapter describes the Babson entrepreneurship ecosystem and how it evolved. However the observations and insights described here can be generalized to many types of schools and efforts to develop entrepreneurship ecosystems.

REFERENCES

Aulet, W. (2008), 'How to build a successful innovation ecosystem: educate, network, and celebrate', *Xconomy.com*, 14 October, available at: http://www.xconomy.com/national/2008/10/14/how-to-built-a-successful-innovation-ecosystem-educate-network-and-celebrate/.

Babson College (2007), *Maintenance of Accreditation Report*, 15 August, AACSB International.

Bygrave, William (ed.) (1993), *The Portable MBA in Entrepreneurship*, New York and Chichester, UK: John Wiley & Sons.

Bygrave, William and Andrew Zacharakis (2007), *Entrepreneurship*, Hoboken, NJ and Chichester, UK: John Wiley & Sons.

Katz, D. and R. Kahn (1978), *The Social Psychology of Organizations, 2nd edn*, New York: John Wiley.

Moore, J.F. (1993), 'Predators and prey: a new ecology of competition', *Harvard Business Review*, May–June, **71** (3): 75–86.

Schein, E. (1983), 'The role of the founder in creating organizational cultures', *Organizational Dynamics,* **12** (1), Summer: 13–28.

Timmons, Jeffry A., Leonard E. Smollen and Alexander L.M. Dingee (1977), *New Venture Creation: A Guide to Small Business Development*, Homewood, IL: R.D. Irwin.

3. EM Lyon Business School

Alain Fayolle and Janice Byrne

The entrepreneurship ecosystem of EM Lyon Business School in 2010 is the culmination of more than 25 years of experience in entrepreneurship education and training. The result is a community of teachers, researchers, students, alumni, entrepreneurs, business leaders, administrative staff and managers committed to the diffusion of an entrepreneurial mindset. The entrepreneurial drive and expertise of the school's human resources have played a considerable role in the creation of this ecosystem. The French business environment and education system have also shaped its emergence and growth. Active engagement with the business sector and the acquisition of appropriate funding have helped the school fuel the development of its ecosystem.

In the pages that follow we describe the facets of the entrepreneurship ecosystem at EM Lyon Business School. We begin with a description of the French context. We then describe the entrepreneurship ecosystem at EM Lyon by outlining its pertinent dimensions: strategy, institutional infrastructure, teaching and learning, outreach initiatives, development and resources. In the third section we chart the development of the school's entrepreneurship ecosystem's development since the 1980s, and conclude with some reflections on the major lessons learned as well as recommendations for schools intent on launching entrepreneurship ecosystems.

THE FRENCH CONTEXT

In this section we document entrepreneurial activity at the national level and offer a brief overview of the higher education system and the current state of entrepreneurship education in France.

Entrepreneurship in France

First coined by Richard Cantillion and later popularized by Jean-Baptiste Say, the term 'entrepreneur' dates back to thirteenth-century France.

Yet today France consistently rates among Europe's poorest performers in entrepreneurial activity (Bosma et al. 2009). Europe's entrepreneurial 'laggard' (Henriquez et al. 2001), France has been said to lack an entrepreneurial culture (Arlotto et al. 2007; Torres and Eminet 2005; Henriquez et al. 2001; Carayannis et al. 2003), and its students are said to have an aversion to entrepreneurship (Arlotto et al. 2007). France rates particularly poorly with respect to high-growth expectation (HEA) entrepreneurial activity. Recent estimates show France exhibiting HEA of under 0.5 percent with less than 10 percent of all start-ups expecting high growth (Bosma et al. 2009). In fact 87 percent of new business creations in 2008 employed only the founding entrepreneur (INSEE 2009). Enterprise creation by higher education graduates remains a marginal phenomenon in France (Fayolle 1999; Béchard 1994), especially when compared to countries such as the United States. While venture creation rates have improved since the 1990s (in 1999, for example, 193 719 business start-ups were recorded compared to 237 000 in 2008), efforts are still needed to stimulate entrepreneurial activity, particularly with high-growth expectation. Explanations for France's low rates of entrepreneurial activity cite structural, geographic, religious, sociological and cultural factors.

Active government intervention – high taxes, red tape and strict regulations – is thought to play a role in stifling the entrepreneurial spirit (Henriquez et al. 2001). The French business environment is characterized by large-scale technology operations and service industries, which can both promote and stifle small and medium-sized enterprise (SME) start-ups. Numerous *groupes d'entreprises* – clusters formed around an activity or region – exist (Henriquez et al. 2001). Most regional clusters account for more than 40 percent of the employment within their region. Innovative and research-intensive SME clusters abound and are often referred to as 'technopoles'. They unite publicly funded research labs, as well as universities and agencies that develop high-technology products and employ highly skilled workers. New businesses and SMEs often gain from joining these clusters because of the opportunities they can derive from spin-off effects, technological dynamism and informational advantages. However the very stakeholders who support the technopoles' existence – large firms, government research centers and educational institutions – may also be said to inhibit the SMEs' development opportunities. The French public research system traditionally avoids contact with the private sector and the university system (Henriquez et al. 2001), and this lack of integration is thought to discourage SME development.

Societal conceptions of what it means to be an entrepreneur do not include the same respect and prestige afforded to the American entrepreneur (Carayannis et al. 2003). The population's aversion to risk and the low tolerance for failure in society are also cited as contributory factors (Torres and Eminet 2005).

The educational system has also been identified as a strong contributory factor. Students envisage permanent positions in large, well-known companies or in the public sector as prestigious and sought-after opportunities. The education system is said to stifle creativity and initiative, and is 'more about producing good employees rather than entrepreneurs' (Torres and Eminet 2005). The French educational system and other environmental factors have thus resulted in a wall that restrains creative expression (Carayannis et al. 2003). The more severe criticisms, however, are reserved for primary and secondary education. Here the professor–student relationship is one of sage and apprentice, and students rarely question what the professor teaches (Carayannis et al. 2003). The educational system tends to place students in streams from a relatively young age, and opportunities to switch at later stages are limited. It has been claimed that the education system is unsuited to the training and education of entrepreneurs (Beranger et al. 1998) and that, in the short term, creating entrepreneurs requires the re-education of students at the undergraduate level (Carayannis et al. 2003).

Before discussing the intricacies of EM Lyon's entrepreneurship ecosystem, we would like to paint a broader picture of the context in which EM Lyon, a highly ranked national *grande école*, operates. To do this we describe the higher education system in France.

Higher Education in France

The French educational system is an established, meritocratic hierarchy. At the tertiary level (undergraduate and above), France is said to have a dual system of education. This means that tertiary education may be obtained through either the traditional state universities or the revered *grandes écoles* ('great schools').

Students who successfully complete their secondary diploma in France have an automatic right to a place at a state university. Tuition fees for these public universities are very low, and there is no (or very limited) selection at entry. Typically this leads to high drop-out rates in the second and third years of university education. The resources devoted to tertiary education have not kept pace with the growth in applicants, and thus the average resources available per student are low (OECD 2007). The more ambitious high school students opt for two years of intense coaching before taking the entrance exam for one of the nation's *grandes écoles* (Barsoux and Lawrence 1991).

Historically the culture of the *grandes écoles* was built on the social and scientific superiority of the elite group they created and reproduced (Henriquez et al. 2001). The overarching objective was to increase the power and influence of these elites within the French economy and society. The *écoles de commerce* (business schools) in the *grande école* tradition were predominantly local institutions set up by the regional business community and financed by the local Chamber of Commerce. They rank among France's most renowned and prestigious educational institutions.

The *grandes écoles* exhibit a number of common characteristics that distinguish them from the state universities:

1. They are small in size and highly selective. Only the top 10 percent of applicants are admitted (Baudelot and Establet 2009).
2. They nurture collaborative ties with the business community.
3. They are autonomous. No national body decides or even coordinates strategies, although to a certain extent the Conferences des Grandes Ecoles (a professional association dedicated to defending the standards and interests of the institutions) encourages cooperation and exchange and provides a system of accreditation.

There is a belief that the value of a *grande école* education does not come from the learning imparted in the schools but rather from the 'rigor of the schools' selection process' (Barsoux and Lawrence 1991, 63). These schools enjoy considerable competitive advantage based on the support they receive from both public and private companies as well as from the managers they train who often recruit from the same schools they attended. Competition among these institutions can be intense, but the need to preserve prestige has generally led to homogeneity in the program offerings at these schools. While available per capita resources vary widely across the system, the more elite institutions spend several times more than the public universities (OECD 2007), and competition for places is fierce.

In recent years the *grandes écoles* have come under increasing criticism. They tend to produce managers who are strong in quantitative thought, analytical abilities, independence and intellectual rigor (Barsoux and Lawrence 1991). The emphasis on selectivity at the entrance level only can have disastrous consequences on the behavior of students during their school years and even on their professional careers. It is argued that this kind of system leads to a form of social elitism: 'the heads of the typical French company were molded by . . . [an educational] system that confirmed their intellectual superiority early in life' (Barsoux and Lawrence 1991, 63). They have also been accused of breeding arrogance: 'senior executives in France believe they owe their high position to their intelligence and cunning' (Barsoux and Lawrence 1991, 62). Another frequently lodged criticism is that these schools produce graduates characterized by an aversion to risk. The quest to be right overrides the creative imperative. In a critique of French *grande école* engineering schools, Veltz (2007) argues that there is too much emphasis on only one criterion for excellence (mathematics), whereas innovation (and thus entrepreneurship) needs a diversity of talents and interpersonal managerial capacities.

Another aspect of the structure of selection and resource allocation is that while the *grandes écoles* attract most of the best students, in the past they have not typically been research-oriented, at least in the business schools, which deprives students of valuable experience and weakens the French research effort. Research has traditionally been located in universities and public research organizations. This situation has evolved recently as some of the *grandes écoles*, both in management and engineering, are associating themselves with universities in centers of excellence (OECD 2007). There is clearly a reason why French students choose to follow this highly competitive and arduous path to higher education. The *grandes écoles* carry a prestigious label. They are characterized by strong alumni networks, they enjoy widely recognized status and reputation, and they generally have better resources and more plentiful capital at their disposal.[1] However there are concerns that these privileges and traditions will not endure in a highly competitive world.

Entrepreneurship Education in France

The stimulation of entrepreneurship in France through education occurs mainly at the tertiary level (Henriquez et al. 2001). However until quite recently France was thought to be lagging in terms of entrepreneurship education (Fayolle 1999). It was not until the late 1990s that entrepreneurship was conceptualized as an important element in the school curriculum (Léger-Jarniou 2001). In 1996 around 30 schools and universities in France offered courses in entrepreneurship or small business management (Fayolle 1997). For the most part, the programs offered were of short duration and more oriented toward enhancing student knowledge of business functions rather than developing their entrepreneurial spirit (Léger-Jarniou 2001). Since the year 2000 both the universities and the *grandes écoles* have made considerable progress with respect to entrepreneurship education (Torres and Eminet 2005; European Commission 2008), and France has been found to perform quite favorably with respect to entrepreneurship education. However there is considerable heterogeneity among the *grandes écoles*, universities and institutions offering entrepreneurship education. Schools differ in terms of culture and practice and there is also a discernible difference between those *grandes écoles* that began investing in the field in the 1980s and those that timidly followed later on (Fayolle 1997).

The focus of this chapter is EM Lyon, an established business school in the *grande école* tradition. The emergence and growth of its entrepreneurship ecosystem must be looked at in the context of both the development of entrepreneurship education in general and the evolution of the broader education system. Three major trends occurring on a globalized level are expected to induce change in the French educational system and more particularly at the *grandes écoles* level. These trends are:

1. internationalization;
2. an increased research focus (French business schools were not previously renowned in this field); and
3. a changing business environment, which means that the job security previously enjoyed by *grande école* graduates may no longer apply (Fendt and Bureau 2010).

In response to these challenges, the French government has adopted initiatives to create more entrepreneurial graduates. The current government actively encourages the educational sector to exploit its resources and expertise to stimulate entrepreneurship teaching and small business creation (Klapper 2004). The development and growth of entrepreneurship education initiatives in France is thus happening at a time of broader systematic change in the educational system. But staunch resistance to change and the imposing legacy of tradition and privilege mean that change – good, bad or indifferent – will not happen overnight. Indeed fighting this deeply engrained sense of what and how tertiary-level education should be conducted in a *grande école* today creates a whole array of problematic issues. The challenge for entrepreneurship educators, who often seek to challenge the status quo or instigate change, is heightened in such an environment. It is against this backdrop that we describe EM Lyon's entrepreneurship ecosystem in the heart of France.

THE ENTREPRENEURSHIP ECOSYSTEM AT EM LYON

Founded in 1872, EM Lyon is a business school rooted in the prestigious *grande école* tradition. As such it benefits from the status, prestige and resources that the *grande école* label confers, but it has also struggled with the bureaucratic, traditional and logical mindset of that label. EM Lyon

Business School is currently recognized as a leader in entrepreneurship education in both France and Europe, a trend that mirrors the blossoming entrepreneurial profile of its surrounding region. Lyon currently ranks among Europe's top 15 cities for entrepreneurship, and the city's local government aims to make the urban area the number one business start-up zone in Europe. EM Lyon plays an active role in the region's development, and the business school, a not-for-profit organization, is affiliated with the Chamber of Commerce and Industry of Lyon. The centrality of its entrepreneurial spirit is illustrated by the school's slogan: 'Educating entrepreneurs for the world'. The spirit of entrepreneurship extends from teaching content to methodologies at both the graduate and the executive level. It also extends to the field of research – two of the school's five research centers are based on a purely entrepreneurship theme – and to the school's outreach activities.

In recent years the school has spread its entrepreneurial roots more widely and now operates one campus in Switzerland (Geneva) and another in China (Shanghai). EM Lyon employs 93 permanent professors plus 36 visiting professors, 30 part-time lecturers, and 25 PhD students and research assistants. Approximately 2700 students attended at undergraduate, postgraduate and doctoral levels in 2009, and over 5000 participate in the school's executive education programs on a yearly basis. One-third of the student population is international, and the school operates partnership agreements with over 100 foreign universities and business schools. In keeping with the school's international orientation, 40 percent of the courses are offered in English.

EM Lyon may be regarded as a *grande école* with a distinctive entrepreneurial and innovative profile. It was one of the first business schools in France to integrate a required course in venture creation for all its undergraduates. It was also one of the first business schools in Europe to gain the Triple Crown accreditation. In the 1990s many of EM Lyon's competitors retained a strong domestic orientation. EM Lyon, however, actively sought international business school partners and forged an international reputation early on. The school attracts more and more international students every year and consistently ranks as Europe's top school for entrepreneurship. EM Lyon is characterized by a vibrant and dynamic entrepreneurship ecosystem which sees entrepreneurship as the common theme underlying diverse school activities. In the following section, we will describe the six dimensions central to the study of entrepreneurship education at this higher level: strategy, teaching and learning efforts, institutional infrastructure, outreach initiatives, development, and resources (European Commission 2008).

Strategy and Leadership

EM Lyon has positioned itself as a world leader in entrepreneurship education. Support from top management is key if the entrepreneurship ecosystem is to succeed as an integral part of the school. EM Lyon's emphasis on entrepreneurship emerged under the leadership of Philippe Albert in the 1980s, and today entrepreneurship continues to play a central role in the school's strategy, as reflected in its slogan. In 2003 Patrick Molle, president of EM Lyon Business School, formalized and updated the centrality of entrepreneurship to the school by launching the 'educating entrepreneurs for the world' initiative. This vision has been at the heart of the institutional strategy ever since. The more years of experience with entrepreneurship education an institution has, the more likely it is to embed entrepreneurship in its mission statement (European Commission 2008). As shown below, EM Lyon has firmly embedded entrepreneurship in its organizational ethos:

> *EM Lyon Business School slogan:* 'Educating entrepreneurs for the world!'
> *EM Lyon Business School mission statement:* 'EM Lyon is a European business school devoted to lifelong learning for entrepreneurial and international management.
>
> Its entrepreneurial and educational project consists of stimulating the social responsibility of its participants, thus giving them all the support needed to achieve business success in the various cultural and economic systems around the world.
>
> Its know-how in training is based both on theory and on day-to-day company management.
>
> Its distinctive quality is founded on teaching innovation and an entrepreneurial approach to management education.'

Educating entrepreneurs for the world is both a mission statement and a strategic objective for EM Lyon. The task of disseminating and upholding this mission is shared by the school's leadership, which is divided among the school president, the dean of the faculty and the dean of academic programs. The president is responsible for the business school strategy, while the dean of faculty and the dean of academic program oversee respectively research and teaching activities, and academic programs such as master's degrees, doctorates and MBAs. It is part of EM Lyon's vision that entrepreneurs and entrepreneurship can have both economic and social value. The school therefore seeks to stimulate social responsibility among its participants, while giving them the support they need to achieve business success in the various cultural and economic systems around the world. Teaching, research and industry-related activities are all guided by this unifying vision.

Teaching and Learning

One of EM Lyon's distinctive capabilities is its emphasis on teaching innovation through an entrepreneurial approach to management education. The teaching staff plays a key role in disseminating the school's entrepreneurial spirit. The school's know-how in entrepreneurship training and education is based on sound theoretical foundations as well as day-to-day practical management experience. It was the school's experience with entrepreneurship coaching in the 1980s and 1990s that created a substantial body of expertise among the school staff. The faculty is organized into four departments: Markets and Innovation; Strategy and Organization; Economics, Finance and Accounting; Management, Law and Human Resources. The entrepreneurship team is housed in the Department of Strategy and Organization, however faculty from all departments teach in the field of entrepreneurship. Some of the key professors now involved in teaching entrepreneurship to undergraduates and graduate students were among the core team of entrepreneur trainers in the early days of the venture creation program offered by the incubation center.

Entrepreneurship education is fully integrated into the curricula for all undergraduate, graduate and postgraduate programs. Students enroll in at least one compulsory course or seminar in entrepreneurship. At the master's, MBA and executive education level, a suite of more specialized courses takes the specific needs of students and executives into account and helps them further develop their entrepreneurial knowledge and competencies. The 2007 launch of the PhD program, which encompasses a specialized entrepreneurship track, further strengthened the school's profile in entrepreneurship research. Courses at the PhD level are important because doctoral students can take advantage of an entrepreneurial mindset as well as skills in their research activities (European Commission 2008). Many of the school's entrepreneurship professors supervise PhD students, which advances their own research on entrepreneurship topics. Examples of course offerings at the respective levels are shown in Box 3.1.

Early educational initiatives at the school revealed that students could only develop entrepreneurial spirit and behavior through an integrated approach. They needed a balanced combination of theory, practice and experimentation. The impact is felt only when the student experiences real engagement in a project and undergoes a period of experimentation, on either an individual or a collective level. Thus the entrepreneurship curriculum at EM Lyon is guided by three main objectives: (1) increasing student awareness of entrepreneurship; (2) improving students' analytical skills and providing tools for the entrepreneurship process; and (3) developing entrepreneurial competencies by engaging in entrepreneurial

---

BOX 3.1   ENTREPRENEURSHIP COURSES AT EM LYON

Bachelor's degree level	Introduction to Entrepreneurship
	Entrepreneurial Team-building
	Programme de Création d'Enterprise (PCE) (Venture Start-up)
	Innovation, Creativity and Entrepreneurship (ICE)
Master's degree level	Entrepreneurial Analysis
	Strategic Management of SMEs
	Business Creation
	Family Business
	New Venture Growth
	Corporate Venturing
	Corporate Entrepreneurship
	Legal and Financial Aspects of Business Creation
	Entrepreneurial Finance
MBA	Market Strategies in the Developing World
	Social Entrepreneurship: Entrepreneurs for the World
	Identifying Entrepreneurial Opportunities
	Evaluating Entrepreneurial Opportunities
	New Venture Growth
	Entrepreneurial Leadership Project
	Corporate Entrepreneurship
Doctoral Level	Entrepreneurship Theories in Action
	Social Entrepreneurship
Executive Education	Intrapreneurship, A Performance Lever
	Innovation Management
	Intrapreneurial Talent Program

---

projects. Objectives 1 and 2 are addressed through the school's program offerings at the graduate and undergraduate levels. Various co-curricular activities also support these objectives (and will be discussed more fully later). To fulfill these objectives, personally engaging pedagogies such as case studies and projects are used. These methods are often considered entrepreneurial pedagogies because they are instrumental in promoting the kind of creativity and openness that underlies the entrepreneurial spirit. The third objective is fulfilled by the incubation center.

Increasing student awareness: the venture start-up project module

In line with the first objective, the school hopes to expose every student to the main issues involved in business start-ups. For example, all incoming undergraduate students are required to enroll in the school's flagship program, the *programme de création d'entreprise* (PCE), or venture start-up project. During this course, students work in teams and take an original idea from conception to (virtual) launch. They learn what is involved in venture creation and the major issues that need to be considered when embarking on an entrepreneurial project. Every year 375 students take this course. They are exposed to traditional lectures on entrepreneurship theory and issues, team-building and creativity modules as well as coaching and group workshops. This course requires significant input from faculty and visiting professors. Faculty from several departments use a team-based approach to teach and coach the student groups, which requires considerable coordination provided by one core member of the entrepreneurship team.

Analytical skills and tools: entrepreneurship courses and electives

This second objective means that students are strongly encouraged to take at least one entrepreneurship course during their master's or MBA program. For example, all students in the different programs take an entrepreneurial analysis course, which places them on the other side of the venture creation process. They analyze the venture through the eyes of would-be evaluators: investors, financiers, clients, accountants, administrators. Students are given the opportunity to analyze complex situations, using tools from other disciplines. Through various project-based assignments, they learn to search and mobilize the necessary resources in their environment to find appropriate solutions to their problems.

Students are also given the option to specialize by choosing from entrepreneurship electives such as family business, corporate entrepreneurship, social entrepreneurship, entrepreneurial finance, business growth, small business management, identifying entrepreneurial opportunities and evaluating entrepreneurial opportunities (see Box 3.1). For these courses, the pedagogical methods mainly involve guided reading, case studies, exposure to guest speakers and class discussion.

Developing practical entrepreneurial competencies: incubator access
Students who have an idea for a new venture and are determined to pursue it may avail themselves of the school's incubator. Pending successful completion of a preliminary evaluation, the entrepreneurial venture and its student promoters are integrated into the incubation center where they can take advantage of individual and group coaching and teaching. In the first six- to 12-month period, students engage in intensive project evaluation and business planning exercises. They learn from their own experiences in a sheltered environment and benefit from working with both internal and external entrepreneurship experts. They build entrepreneurial networks as well as their knowledge base in the requisite marketing, legal, financial and operational aspects of the business. Once the business is brought to fruition, students may also benefit from a final business development and reporting stage, which continues for 24 months. The incubation center is paramount to the entrepreneurship ecosystem's development, and we will discuss its functioning in more detail in the next section.

Institutional Infrastructures

An effective entrepreneurship ecosystem entails parallel actions in a number of areas. Institutional infrastructure encompasses the facilities that support entrepreneurship education, such as an entrepreneurship center or an incubator, as well as the people appointed to run such facilities, for instance entrepreneurship professors. These elements also cover research and cross-disciplinary structures that further support and develop entrepreneurship education at the institution (European Commission 2008). Some of the institutional infrastructures that support entrepreneurship education and its development at EM Lyon are outlined below. We make reference to long-standing entities such as the entrepreneurship research centers and the incubator and describe the entrepreneurship professors and staff that work in them.

Research in entrepreneurship
EM Lyon Business School is increasingly recognized as a world leader in entrepreneurship education. One reason for this reputation is the growing prominence of its research outcomes. The school is regularly identified as a key partner for external institutions that are undertaking research initiatives. The school was identified early on as the French partner for the Global Entrepreneurship Monitor (GEM) and more recently as the French partner for the Global University Entrepreneurial Spirits Students Survey (GUESSS[2]). Entrepreneurship researchers at the school also engage in research projects for the French Ministry of Industry and Commerce, the

Organisation for Economic Co-operation and Development (OECD), the National Institute of Statistics and Economic Studies (INSEE), and the European Commission. Research centers are collectives of faculty members who, together with PhD students and corporate partners (both not-for-profit and for-profit organizations), develop an ambitious disciplinary or interdisciplinary research program in accordance with the general mission of the school. Currently EM Lyon houses five institutes and research centers, two of which – the Entrepreneurial Processes Dynamics Research Center and the New Venture Creation and Growth Research Center – are devoted purely to entrepreneurship. Plans for a future research institute, the European Institute of Entrepreneurship, are also under way.

The Entrepreneurial Processes Dynamics[3] Research Center was established in 2005. Its research focuses on four key areas: processes leading to the creation and growth of innovative enterprises; corporate entrepreneurship; entrepreneurship education; and the evaluation of public policies in terms of business creation and revival. The center currently houses an average of ten researchers and ten PhD students. Researchers in the center hold editorial positions on numerous referenced entrepreneurship journals and publish scientific articles, books and book chapters as well as case studies about their research. The center's professors often engage in research at the request of institutions (OECD), other academic partners (Babson, University of St-Gallen) and governments (France, Sweden) and also regularly appear as keynote speakers at international conferences and events on the topic of entrepreneurship.

A second entrepreneurship research center, the New Venture Creation and Growth Research Center, was created in 2007 under the direction of Frédéric Delmar. Its purpose is to address specific research questions about the new venture creation process and the growth of young firms. As of 2009 the center employed five professors and ten PhD students are working at this center. Their research focuses on four main areas: the strategies of venture capital firms in developing countries; the role of venture capital firms in regional development; the impact of regional policies on cohorts of new firms; and the dynamics of high-growth start-ups. The center works with partner schools in Russia and Sweden and relies mostly on large longitudinal databases for its research. Under the initiative and supervision of this center, a weekly entrepreneurship research seminar has been in operation since 2007. This seminar – faithfully attended by PhD students, faculty and visiting professors alike – facilitates research collaboration and idea exchange as members meet to present and discuss their findings.

Plans for the development of a new research center, the European

Institute of Entrepreneurship, are currently under way. This research center is a joint initiative with EM Lyon's Chinese partner, Zhejiang University. The joint research center will host a postdoctoral student from Zhejiang University as well as a student from EM Lyon's PhD program. Researchers are expected to work closely with Frédéric Delmar's research center (New Venture Creation and Growth) on joint research that specifically addresses entrepreneurship in the context of developing countries. As the size and resources of research entities become increasingly important for international competition, EM Lyon Business School plans to merge its entrepreneurship research centers in the near future. A central forum for European entrepreneurship researchers is a powerful concept but it requires significant resources and coordination. This will be one of the major challenges facing the ecosystem in the years to come.

The incubator at the Entrepreneurship Center
The incubator at EM Lyon (originally known as the Entrepreneurship Center) is at the heart of every aspect of the school's entrepreneurial activity. Since 1984 more than 600 companies and 10 000 jobs have been created there. The incubator maintains strong links with the internal teaching departments, entrepreneurship professors and researchers as well as with the external structures that provide helpful resources like funding, intellectual capital and networks.

In June 2008, more than 20 years after its inception, the long-established incubator was revitalized. Tagged the 'new-generation incubator', it now offers a longer-term structural support that integrates four key services: teaching; coaching and mentoring; networking; and infrastructure aid. The revamped incubation center offers two programs: the start-up program (directed at participants with new business creation projects) and the takeover program (directed at participants who have recently taken over an existing firm). Departing from its previous emphasis on external clients, the revitalized incubator is now available for projects by EM Lyon students. Thirteen potential projects will be given the chance to operate from the incubator center. Potential targets include start-ups based on high technology, service innovation or with a strong social orientation. The new-generation incubator focuses on group dynamics and the exchange of experience. As before, facilitators make use of targeted teaching methods and facilitate interactions between participants and experienced entrepreneurs.

The school has also created an online social network dedicated to a community of entrepreneurs, the Agora EM Lyon Incubator. It is the first of its kind because it is a social network that revolves solely around the school. In line with Web 2.0 technologies and similar to Facebook,

Viadeo or LinkedIn, this entrepreneurial hub seeks to provide a platform for exchange, discussion, business opportunities and commercial visibility, while giving members access to a range of information useful to entrepreneurs. The Agora EM Lyon Incubator also includes a blog, a NetVibes page and a widget. Numerous people associated with EM Lyon – entrepreneurs within the incubator, enterprise partners, students, professors, coaches and incubator alumni – can access and use the network.

EM Lyon's steady accumulation of world-class research and practice in entrepreneurship has enabled the school to increase its visibility and instigate a number of outreach initiatives. These outreach activities in turn affirm the school's role as a premier entrepreneurship institution. Some of the school's outreach activities are outlined in the subsequent section.

Outreach Activities

There are many stakeholders who play a key role in the entrepreneurship ecosystem at EM Lyon. These stakeholders include students, faculty, alumni, investors, entrepreneurs, school management, research centers, industry, and community and regional representatives. Outreach involves the entrepreneurship co-curricular and extracurricular activities and events organized for EM Lyon's internal and external stakeholders. Two of the major outreach activities driven by faculty and staff – the incubation center and research – have already been discussed. The incubation center cements EM Lyon's important role of stimulating entrepreneurial activity. Its recent revamp means that the incubation center now addresses both internal and external stakeholders. The research centers constitute another major outreach activity. Because of the links between the research centers and industry, local entrepreneurs, partner institutions and government bodies, EM Lyon continues to fulfill its strategic mission while maintaining its visibility. Other outreach events and activities not previously mentioned are outlined below.

Outreach activities in the business community
Mirroring the entrepreneurial behavior that the school hopes to transmit, EM Lyon boasts an impressive social network. The school has strong links with industry and business and relies on these relationships to invigorate its teaching and resource base. The school nurtures close ties with well-established businesses vis-à-vis numerous research and funding initiatives. It enjoys funding and sponsorship from some of France's largest financial, media and research institutions. EM Lyon has external partners for most of its entrepreneurship education programs. They include successful entrepreneurs, bankers, venture capitalists, business angels, consultants

and public agencies. External partners are relied upon to finance, advise and support EM Lyon's initiatives and ongoing programs. Two concrete examples of such initiatives within the business community include the school's 'Learning from Entrepreneurs' conference series and its involvement in the region's Salon for Entrepreneurs' conventions.

Every month, EM Lyon welcomes top speakers to share their experiences and thoughts on themes relevant to the school's entrepreneurial mission. The 'Learning from Entrepreneurs' conference series offers a unique opportunity for debate and exchange between students and the broader business world. Recent speakers have included high-ranking executives from TNT, Danone, Ferrari, Nestlé and Michelin, as well as the Turkish Minister for Industry and the president of Olympique Lyonnais, a popular soccer team. This event has enjoyed sponsorship by *Figaro*, a leading French newspaper.

EM Lyon Business School contributes every year to the Salon des Entrepreneurs, Lyon Rhône-Alpes, a regional convention that provides a meeting place and information center for anyone interested in entrepreneurship. Those attending include current and future entrepreneurs, inventors, franchisers, financers, investors, SME managers, students and the unemployed. The goal is to create a place where potential entrepreneurs can make contact with potential collaborators and investors or learn about the most up-to-date legal and financial regulations. The 2009 convention included almost 100 workshops, 150 exhibitors, 400 experts and ten key note speakers and attracted almost 15000 visitors. EM Lyon's active role in the convention legitimizes its role as a center of training and education for entrepreneurs and its position as a key force in the development of regional business.

Outreach activities in the local community

EM Lyon emphasizes the importance of creating social value and tries to ensure that teaching and research activities reflect this principle. In recent years concrete efforts to affirm the school's role in creating social value in its own environment have resulted in several outreach events and associations. One is the Entrepreneurs in the City project. It was launched in 2007 in association with Sports in the City, a charity that targets disadvantaged youth. Participants in this program, who come from disadvantaged areas of the Rhône-Alpes region, have a preliminary business idea. Once accepted in the program, they benefit from three months of tailored entrepreneurship training and coaching at EM Lyon provided by the school's experienced staff at the Entrepreneurship Center. The program culminates in a competition where prizes are awarded for best overall project, best business plan and best idea.

Afterwards participants are eligible for follow-up support from experts in various domains (law, insurance, accounting, communication and marketing) who offer the kind of advice and counsel that would be difficult to come by otherwise. After completing the program, participants also benefit from advantageous credit terms offered by some of the region's premier banking institutions.[4] Since the program's inception in 2007, 31 young founders have been supported in business creation; 16 have since started their own businesses, and six are in the process of doing so. There were 19 participants in the third cohort of this innovative new program.

Outreach activities on an international level
A recent outreach event of particular importance was the World Entrepreneurship Forum (WEF). Launched in 2008, the WEF is the first worldwide think-tank dedicated to entrepreneurs and their role in society. It was established by EM Lyon Business School in collaboration with KPMG. The goal of WEF is to produce and disseminate recommendations for building a world where the 'entrepreneur is key in the creation of wealth and social justice'. It comprises 96 members representing 35 nationalities. The yearly forum supports the school's 'educating entrepreneurs for the world' strategy, and it also facilitates the exchange of knowledge, ideas and experiences among entrepreneurship academics, entrepreneurs, experts and politicians. Key topics include policy measures, the 'green' entrepreneur, the corporate entrepreneur, women entrepreneurs, taking the plunge from employee to entrepreneur, micro credit and micro assurance, as well as entrepreneurship and the local community. The first WEF took place in Evian, France, on 13–15 November 2008. It gathered 72 participants from 35 countries and over 300 attended its gala celebration. The 2008 forum received the support of the French Senate, Assemblée Nationale, the Department of Research and Education, as well as that of the OECD. The forum's patronage by President Nicolas Sarkozy of France is testament to the importance and timeliness of such an initiative for the international community. The 2009 forum assembled 80 members from over 40 countries and specifically addressed the role of the government in supporting entrepreneurship in times of crisis. The next forum, scheduled for November 2010, will once again bring together world experts, academics and entrepreneurs to share and exchange ideas on entrepreneurship.

Alumni outreach events
The school continuously capitalizes on its strong alumni network. True to its *grande école* tradition, EM Lyon benefits from an active alumni network with over 16 600 members. EM Lyon alumni who have started

companies or had other entrepreneurial experiences are invited to return as lecturers and guest speakers. Other alumni activities within the eco-system include hiring graduates, sponsoring internships and alumni feed-back on student ideas, opportunities and plans. The alumni association publishes a monthly newsletter (*L'essentiel*), which contains personal entrepreneurial success stories of EM Lyon graduates as well as informa-tion about meetings and business breakfasts and dinners with successful entrepreneurs.

Outreach involving other institutions and partner schools

In accordance with its international strategy base, EM Lyon enjoys part-nerships with a number of domestic and foreign educational establish-ments. Past and current partner schools include the Aston Business School (Birmingham, UK), LMU (Munich, Germany), the University of Texas (Austin, USA), York University (Canada), University of Connecticut (Storrs, USA), Aston University (UK) and Pace University (New York, USA). The school's recent collaboration with Babson and Zhejiang University resulted in the new Global Entrepreneurship Program in 2008. This program combines three continents and three business schools with one focus and seeks to capitalize on the world's best entrepreneurial teach-ing in three diverse global markets to prepare students for global entrepre-neurial careers.

On the domestic front, EM Lyon announced a new collaboration with a neighboring engineering school, l'Ecole Centrale de Lyon, in July 2009. By partnering with Ecole Centrale de Lyon, EM Lyon expects to realize considerable cross-discipline collaboration. Cross-discipline structures are said to be conducive to effective entrepreneurial education (European Commission 2008). Both schools hope to build synergies by combining their respective scientific and business bases. There are also plans to build a common campus, which should stimulate curricular innovation, allow for sharing executive education and accentuate international coopera-tion and alliances. The laboratories of l'Ecole Centrale de Lyon and EM Lyon's incubator are seen as potential centers of business and engineering synergy.

Development

Program development covers the way in which an institution develops its entrepreneurship activities and the staff involved in the teaching of entre-preneurship. This dimension consists of three subdimensions: evaluation; user-driven improvement; and human resources development and man-agement (European Commission 2008).

Evaluation
Because entrepreneurship is at the heart of EM Lyon's strategy, key indicators focus on the business school's reputation and international rankings in the field of entrepreneurship. In the 2009 *Financial Times* European Business school rankings, EM Lyon appears as the eighth-ranked business school in Europe and the first in entrepreneurship. Another important indicator is the school's attractiveness (based on its entrepreneurship profile) as reported by students or others applying to the school. In recent years, the Programme de Création d'Entreprise (Program for Business Creation or PCE) at the bachelor's level has become a flagship program for the school, and potential candidates often cite it as a significant 'pull' factor in entry-level interviews. EM Lyon also pays a great deal of attention to the number of students who choose entrepreneurship electives. In the master's programs, one in three students (more than 500) choose at least one entrepreneurship course as an elective. Between 2006 and 2009 the number of students interested in pursuing an entrepreneurial track that offers numerous entrepreneurship electives doubled. Empirical investigation also confirms that the school's 'educating entrepreneurs for the world' initiative supports the development of an entrepreneurial mindset and orientation among students in addition to business start-ups and the growth of firms. The incubator keeps in touch with previous program participants and monitors their performance. As previously mentioned, more than 600 companies have been formed since the incubator's inception in 1984. Almost 90 percent of those companies are still in existence five years after their involvement in the program.

User-driven improvement
Curriculum improvement is often triggered by students. At the end of an entrepreneurship course, students are asked to give their opinion about whether the course achieved its stated objectives and about its content, and the methods and entrepreneurial expertise of the lecturers and speakers. These comments are then fed back to departmental heads. The course coordinator for the core PCE course integrated student feedback, comments and suggestions over the years, and now the course has one of the school's highest satisfaction rankings. Because EM Lyon is strongly engaged in entrepreneurship education research, students are often the source of empirical investigations. The results of the research are regularly incorporated into course content or used to trigger a change in pedagogy. Most of the current development at EM Lyon is user-driven as opposed to driven by evaluations from end-users (investors, employers and so on). This is a matter of consideration for future development within the school.

Human resources development and management

Entrepreneurship teaching at institutions of higher education in Europe is often carried out by faculty who have limited personal experience with entrepreneurship (European Commission 2008). EM Lyon defies this norm since many of its entrepreneurship professors either have direct experience with business start-ups (many started their own companies and later turned to academia) or are heavily involved in the incubation center's coaching and mentoring activities, which gives them a rich base of experience they can use in their everyday teaching.

To recruit its highly qualified and international personnel in entrepreneurship, EM Lyon relies heavily on personal networks. The growing visibility of the school as one of Europe's premier educational institutions in entrepreneurship means that academics in this area naturally gravitate toward it. Once they are recruited, it is important to retain team members, a task made all the more difficult by the competitive academic market. Entrepreneurship professors are therefore allocated challenging and high-profile pedagogical and research responsibilities, for example complete responsibility for the school's flagship venture start-up program (Frédéric Delmar), leadership of the school's research connections with Chinese academic partners (Saulo Barbosa), and curricula innovation based on prior research (Ignasi Marti).

Resources

Financial resources: private and public funding

Dedicated funding is imperative to the survival of any entrepreneurship ecosystem. Without the necessary resources, activities such as appointing professors, developing courses, establishing an entrepreneurial center or arranging extracurricular activities for the students would be impossible (European Commission 2008). As a result EM Lyon set up the Entrepreneurs for the World Foundation. This foundation contributes to the funding of major projects that are compatible with the school's mission statement. All the selected projects must represent a significant step forward in the field of entrepreneurship. The global and multifaceted foundation supports efforts to raise awareness of the entrepreneurial spirit of the campus and to promote micro-credit and quality research programs proposed by its centers and institutes. The main selection criterion is the quality of the proposed project, with a clear preference given to the promotion of the role of the entrepreneur in the world.

The annual budget for entrepreneurship activities of approximately €1.5 million is covered by the Entrepreneurs for the World Foundation, in tandem with funding from private companies and public funds.[5] The share of private financing is over 60 percent. Private financial partners are generally interested in one program or one structure that could be used to reinforce their corporate communication strategy. The majority of incubator financing comes from three founding partners and 18 associate partners. The establishment of endowed chairs is another powerful way to favor research within schools. They also constitute an important strategic tool for companies. Chairs within schools in France are generally initiated by professional associations or organizations and generally involve sponsorship of a research project for at least three years, which in some instances is renewable. EM Lyon works with the Caisse d'Epargne Rhône-Alpes (a regional banking institution) to investigate the financial practices of growth firms and with Cegid Group to research innovation in information systems.

Human resources: entrepreneurship teaching corps
The 'educating entrepreneurs for the world' approach is strongly dependent on human resources and culture. A key element in EM Lyon's strategy has been to recruit and integrate highly qualified entrepreneurship professors. A recent study commissioned by the European Union found that schools in Europe that had more than 12 years of experience in entrepreneurship education had, on average, 2.6 entrepreneurship professors employed at the school (European Commission 2008). In the academic year 2009/10 EM Lyon employed nine professors (full, associate and assistant) in entrepreneurship. In line with the school's international orientation, an emphasis is also placed on international recruitment. Thirty percent of the faculty is of foreign nationality, and this rises to 50 percent in the entrepreneurship faculty.

One of the school's distinctive capabilities is its emphasis on teaching innovation and its entrepreneurial approach to management education. This know-how in training is based on a sound theoretical foundation as well as day-to-day practical management experience. The school's foray into entrepreneurship training in the 1980s and 1990s resulted in a substantial body of expertise among the school staff. Some of the foremost professors currently teaching entrepreneurship to undergraduates and graduate students were among the core team of entrepreneur-trainers in the early days of the venture creation program. Their practical experience supporting and coaching entrepreneurs during the everyday struggles of business creation enrich their teaching at EM Lyon.

Human and financial resources have clearly played a key role in creating the entrepreneurship ecosystem at EM Lyon today. Without them the teaching, learning, research and incubation facilities would not exist. The strategic commitment of school leaders, coupled with outreach and development initiatives, have succeeded in affirming EM Lyon's visibility and strength in entrepreneurship education. These elements of the ecosystem are nourished by an overarching entrepreneurial culture, but an organizational culture takes time to develop. A historical inquiry into the development of EM Lyon's entrepreneurship ecosystem is therefore essential in explaining its emergence. Interviews with past and previous school leaders, entrepreneurship professors and administrative staff helped paint this historical picture. We supplemented these accounts by reviewing relevant media and press releases as well as school brochures and documentation.

ENTREPRENEURSHIP ECOSYSTEM DEVELOPMENT

Throughout the course of its development, EM Lyon has been both a vector and an engine of innovation and entrepreneurial spirit in its region. Since its founding by businessmen in the silk industry in 1872, entrepreneurship has been sewn into the very fabric of the school. Today, EM Lyon is one of France's, and Europe's, leading business schools. The activities and initiatives that characterized the development of EM Lyon's entrepreneurship ecosystem since the 1980s are described below.

Ecosystem Emergence and Experimentation: EM Lyon in the 1980s

EM Lyon, formerly known as the Ecole Supérieure de Commerce de Lyon or ESC Lyon, was one of the first business schools in France to embrace entrepreneurship pedagogy and research. The integration of entrepreneurship into the school curriculum can be traced to the early 1980s and the innovative efforts of Philippe Albert. At their start many entrepreneurship initiatives hinge on the determination and passion of one or more influential people (Kuratko 2005). It was Philippe Albert and the entrepreneurial team he created that would drive the school's development and pave an innovative path for other French business schools to follow. Albert was educated at the Ecole des Hautes Etudes Commerciales de Paris (HEC Paris) and INSEAD and was experienced in both SME and multinational business. Prior to Albert's recruitment, EM Lyon had been a well-known *grande école* that offered general management education. However a challenging business environment and increasing competition signaled the need for change. Albert's mission was to internationalize the school and advance its competitive position. Following the successful launch of an international MBA program, Albert endeavored to differentiate the school, forge more links with the business community and contribute to the region's development. To accomplish this he set about guiding the school's active engagement in empirical SME and management research.

The Entrepreneurship Center was founded in 1984. It was created by Albert with the objective of encouraging entrepreneurship inside as well as outside the school. Albert felt its physical location within the heart of the school was an important symbol for students. He wanted them to be aware of the real-life entrepreneurial projects that were taking place in their midst.

In 1984 the school formally launched the Progamme d'Appui (Venture Support Program). It was delivered by the Entrepreneurship Center and would become the school's flagship program. The Venture Support Program was a key driver in the institutionalization of entrepreneurship at EM Lyon. It was targeted at the school's external community and was delivered via the EM Lyon Entrepreneurship (later Incubator) Center. Participants followed practical business courses in law, marketing and finance while also benefiting from personalized coaching and financial support. The local (Rhône-Alpes) development agency sponsored the participation of potential entrepreneurs in the six-month program as a way to foster economic growth and ease unemployment in the region. A dedicated team of business coaches and mentors from the school nurtured and supported local business people who had ideas and start-up aspirations. As the program's popularity and recognition grew, so too did the entrepreneurial expertise and pedagogical know-how of the entrepreneurship teaching team.

EM Lyon tentatively began to extend its entrepreneurial teaching, training and coaching expertise to the school's internal audience. Support initiatives were increasingly offered to undergraduate, master's level and MBA students within the school. At the outset these initiatives primarily consisted of inviting entrepreneurs to be guest speakers and offering courses that aimed to raise students' awareness of entrepreneurship. However the potential of such efforts to mobilize student entrepreneurial activity soon became evident, and in 1985 a second Venture Support Program was proposed for local undergraduate, master's and MBA students as well as for students from the nearby engineering school. This second-generation Venture Support Program was created to favor the growth of actual business start-ups based on students' ideas. The year 1985 also saw the creation of an endowed chair for business creation supported by Lyonnaise de Banque. This chair gave professors from different departments the opportunity to formalize teaching methods, classes, cases and research avenues. In 1986 a third program, the campus seminar, was created. Its goal was to raise awareness among the academic and scientific community of the issues, opportunities and constraints of entrepreneurship research.

The week-long seminar was enthusiastically received by students, doctoral students, professors and researchers, who in some cases signed up with the Venture Support Program to initiate their own projects.

Ecosystem Expansion and Growth: EM Lyon in the 1990s

The second wave of entrepreneurship education took place in the 1990s as EM Lyon began to build on its past experience and redefined and developed its activities and strategy. From 1991 onward the school progressively broadened its entrepreneurship course offerings. An entrepreneurship elective was proposed for MBA students, and two years later a similar elective was offered to third-year undergraduates. In 1994 a number of entrepreneurship courses were created that enabled undergraduates to choose an entrepreneurship stream composed of three entrepreneurship courses. In 1996 the school introduced a major innovation: for the first time, all first-year undergraduates at EM Lyon (approximately 300 students) were involved in a compulsory venture creation project. In teams of five, students had to develop a project and build a business plan. This kind of module was relatively new at the time, and its integration as a compulsory course for first-year students was especially innovative.

As previously mentioned, engagement in research was not traditionally viewed as part of the *grande école* tradition in France. Research was traditionally (and to an extent still is) carried out by government bodies and removed from educational institutions. Teaching and research were not usually housed within the same institution. In 1992, however, EM Lyon set up a research center within the school. Known as IRE (Institut de recherche de l'entreprise, or the Enterprise Research Institute), it was financed by outside businesses and private companies, which was extremely innovative for the time. The IRE comprised four to five small research teams, each grouped around its area of interest, and members simultaneously engaged in teaching and active field research. The research that was produced was practically relevant and scientifically rigorous; its output was teachable. IRE became central to the school's functioning and constituted a real departure from the *grande école* tradition, which typically discouraged academic and industry collaboration. One of the IRE subteams was devoted solely to research on SMEs. Much of its research was sponsored by the Ministry of Commerce and Industry with the objective of shedding more light on what kinds of SMEs existed and how the government could assist in their development. This team would later prove to be the kernel of expertise for the school's expansion into entrepreneurship education and research.

In 1997 the IRE was reconceptualized under a school restructuring scheme, and the team of researchers devoted to investigating SMEs set up their own specialized Centre des Entrepreneurs or Entrepreneurship Center. This new center began to work more closely with those involved in the flagship Venture Support Program, and synergies between research and teaching were quickly realized.

Throughout its development, EM Lyon has been particularly open to its surroundings and external stakeholders. In 1993, the school launched a program called Entreprendre Pour Se Reconvertir (Entrepreneurship to Change One's Career) to sensitize older executives to the entrepreneurship process. Its goal was to help them assess their career trajectory and verify whether they had the necessary competencies and desire to start their own businesses. In 1996 this program was modified and delivered to Air France personnel as part of an ambitious staff conversion program.

In 1998 EM Lyon obtained unconditional European Quality Improvement System (EQUIS) accreditation, which was renewed in 2003 and again in 2008. EM Lyon was one of the first business schools in Europe to become voluntarily involved in the accreditation process.

In the 1980s and 1990s the school was experimenting with its entrepreneurial ethos. Its entrepreneurship education and training for both internal and external customers, coupled with its focus on research, were considered extremely innovative for the time. Throughout this period, Albert viewed the school's Entrepreneurship Center as crucial to the development of entrepreneurship education. Two essential aspects of the Entrepreneurship Center are worthy of note. First and foremost it acted as an incubator to nurture and support business start-ups. The center accompanied and supported entrepreneurs in venture creation, takeovers and development. In its first 12 years of existence, the center assisted almost 300 projects through the Venture Support Program. A total of 143 companies that participated in this program were still in existence five years later, and they created almost 1000 new positions. The second aspect of the Entrepreneurship Center encompasses its position as a research and pedagogical engineering center. Teaching benefited from the real-world interactions and exchanges among entrepreneurs, students and professors. A team of three professors who specialized in entrepreneurship ran the laboratory and research center and coordinated over 30 professors from different departments throughout the school. The center houses a permanent team of over ten researchers. An overview of some key events in the growth of the school's ecosystem is outlined in Box 3.2.

Ecosystem Scaling: EM Lyon Enters the New Millennium

The early years of the new millennium witnessed a further legitimization of the role of entrepreneurship at EM Lyon. The year 2003 marked the

---

BOX 3.2   EM LYON ECOSYSTEM TIMELINE

1984 Entrepreneurship chair created
      Launch of Entrepreneurship Center and *appui* program
1985 Launch of student-oriented *appui* program
1986 Creation of CAMPUS program
1992 IRE research center established
      Entrepreneurship elective offered to MBA and third-year
      undergraduate students
1993 Launch of manager-to-entrepreneur conversion program
1994 Entrepreneurship stream introduced for bachelor's
      students
1995 Launch of family enterprise program
      Alumni network set up
1996 Compulsory PCE introduced
1997 ESC 125th birthday
      Renamed EM Lyon
1998 Obtained EQUIS accreditation
2003 Strategic initiative 'Creating Entrepreneurs for the World'
      EM Lyon joins Maison de l'Entrepreneuriat
2004 EM Lyon opens Shanghai campus
2006 Launch of PhD program with entrepreneurship track
2007 Launch of Entrepreneurs in the City program
2008 EM Lyon ranked first in entrepreneurship by *Financial
      Times*
      WEF
      Global entrepreneurship program

---

beginning of 'Entrepreneurs for the World', an initiative that emphasized the centrality of entrepreneurship in the school's strategy. This initiative led to several others in the years to come, which reinforced the school's visibility as a premier provider of entrepreneurship education and training. Some of the resulting initiatives have already been discussed. A brief overview of the important developments is presented below.

In 2003 the Entrepreneurship Center (incubator) joined the Maison de l'Entrepreneuriat (House of Entrepreneurship), an association charged with uniting French universities and *grandes écoles* that were interested in stimulating an entrepreneurial spirit in their students. Three years later EM Lyon launched its own PhD program to produce top-quality researchers and teachers in the area of management and entrepreneurship.

PhD students engaged in entrepreneurship research benefit from their proximity to world-class researchers and professors in entrepreneurship.

Another objective has been to deepen the school's engagement in the community and its contribution to regional development. In 2007 a new program, Entrepreneurs in the City, was launched. This program symbolizes the school's view of entrepreneurship, which goes beyond the economic implications. In collaboration with a well-known local association that uses sports to help disadvantaged youth (Sports in the City), the program's aim is to promote and support business start-ups by young entrepreneurs from disadvantaged backgrounds.

July 2009 saw the revamp of the school's Entrepreneurship Incubation Center. The mission of this second-generation incubator is to increase services to the internal (student) community while also offering an online social networking forum for its numerous collaborators, participants and external stakeholders.

The first decade of the new millennium has also seen EM Lyon reach out to create more international partnerships and extend its influence. The World Entrepreneurship Forum (previously described) was first launched in November 2008 and plans are currently under way for the 2010 forum. In February 2009 the school finalized another important partnership. EM Lyon Business School, Babson College's F.W. Olin Graduate School of Business and Zhejiang University's School of Management joined forces to develop a master's degree in global entrepreneurship that began in autumn 2009. Three of the world's leading institutions in the field of entrepreneurship have united to provide the first global entrepreneurship program to be carried out on three continents.

The school's efforts to bolster its position as a leader in entrepreneurship education have been recognized. In September 2008 the *Financial Times* ranked EM Lyon as the number one business school in entrepreneurship. Two months later the *Financial Times* ranked EM Lyon number eight among the top 65 European business schools.

REFLECTIONS ON EM LYON'S ENTREPRENEURSHIP ECOSYSTEM

Lessons Learned

Importance of strategic commitment

A review of EM Lyon's ecosystem highlights some key success factors in its development. The school's strategic commitment, the centrality of entrepreneurship to its vision and the commitment of its leadership have all meant that 'educating entrepreneurs for the world' is more than just a catchy slogan. Recent strategic projects such as the Global Entrepreneurship Program, the second-generation Incubation Center and the plans for the new (merged) Entrepreneurship Research Center underscore this commitment. Infrastructural entities like the research centers and the incubator are instrumental to the ecosystem's vitality and survival. Entrepreneurship is embedded in the school's strategic mission and therefore has become a guiding light for every major action, initiative and decision by the school's leaders. It is the persistent strategic vision of the school's leaders, from Philippe Albert in the 1980s to Patrick Molle today, that explain the continued success of EM Lyon's entrepreneurship ecosystem.

Mobilizing and transferring entrepreneurial experience
The smooth functioning of institutional infrastructures can be attributed to the commitment and drive of the entrepreneurship professors and administrative staff that constitute them. At EM Lyon, 25 years of experience coaching budding entrepreneurs via the incubator has been mobilized as a source of competitive advantage. The expertise and knowledge that faculty gained from meeting and counseling entrepreneurs from the external community was later transferred to the school's internal audience.

Retaining core members of the entrepreneurship team is therefore an important challenge in today's competitive academic market. Special attention has to be paid to these key resources in the success of EM Lyon's entrepreneurship strategy. This has been accomplished by offering professors challenging and rewarding pedagogical and research responsibilities. In the future the school must continue to renew its entrepreneurial pedagogy by training and educating educators.

Creating an entrepreneurial culture
Activities, initiatives and decisions made in six key areas (strategy; teaching and learning; institutional infrastructures; outreach activities; resources; and development) explain the entrepreneurship ecosystem that exists at EM Lyon Business School today. We believe that the organizational culture is the overarching ethos that informs and influences these decisions and activities (see Figure 3.1). An effective entrepreneurship ecosystem thrives on a common entrepreneurial mindset. Organizational culture is one of the most potent sources of this mindset.

It is these forces combined – the strategic vision, the embedded know-how and the pervasive entrepreneurial culture – that have nourished the emergence and growth of EM Lyon's entrepreneurship ecosystem. No single dimension of the ecosystem – resources, teaching expertise

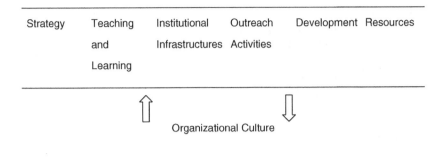

Figure 3.1   Key areas that create organizational culture

or research capabilities – explains the school's current lead. Rather it is the systematic coherence of the various dimensions, underpinned by the organizational culture, which has resulted in the sustainable and successful entrepreneurship ecosystem of today.

Recommendations

Business schools must strive to ensure that there is sufficient strategic commitment to the creation and development of an entrepreneurship ecosystem. In practice this means that the educational institution must be prepared to evaluate every activity and decision in light of the guiding strategic objective. Decisions on funding, academic partners, curricular innovation and research directions must follow a coherent pattern that embodies and emboldens the entrepreneurship ecosystem.

Entrepreneurship research is a key dimension in the institutional strategy of EM Lyon Business School. The biggest challenge is to facilitate the integration of entrepreneurship research results into entrepreneurship education and pedagogy. In order to do this, research should systematically address practical and pedagogical issues, and entrepreneurship research should be tightly connected to societal needs and demands. Schools should consider research initiatives that enhance and reinforce the school's entrepreneurship ecosystem.

Innovative attempts to mobilize entrepreneurial expertise and transfer it to the classroom must be pursued. This implies drawing on internal staff as well as external contacts (current entrepreneurs and experienced alumni) to enrich the students' learning experience. Efforts must be made to retain core staff, who embody valuable pedagogical experience and entrepreneurial vision.

Educational institutions seeking to create an entrepreneurship eco-system must design an integrated ecosystem system, a system in which strategy, infrastructure, teaching and learning, outreach activities, development and resources all work together to form a coherent whole. This system's cohesiveness relies on a strong organizational culture and a pervasive entrepreneurial mindset.

NOTES

1. The best French business schools (such as EM Lyon) are at the top of the European rankings and their master's degree programs have a reputation of excellence in Europe based on regular surveys and the records of the *Financial Times*.
2. GUESSS is an initiative run by the university of St-Gallen in Switzerland and the European Business School. It helps systematically record the venture-founding intentions and activity of students on a long-term basis, and makes temporal and geographical comparisons possible.
3. Under the directorship of Professor Alain Fayolle.
4. Partners include Adie, Siparex, PricewaterhouseCoopers and the Caisse d'Epargne Rhône-Alpes.
5. The budget presented here does not take into consideration the salaries and related costs for teaching, research and outreach activities.

REFERENCES

Arlotto, Jacques, Jean-Pierre Boissin and Stephan Maurin (2007), 'L'intention entrepreneuriale des étudiants Grandes Ecoles/Universités: un faux débat?' ('Entrepreneurial intention of Grande Ecole and University Students: a false debate?') Paper presented at the 5th Congrès Internationale de l'Académie de l'Entpreneuriat.

Barsoux, J.L. and P. Lawrence (1991), 'The making of a French manager', *Harvard Business Review*, July–August: 58–67.

Baudelot, C. and R. Establet (2009), *L'elitisme républicain. L'Ecole française à L'epreuve des comparaisons internationals*, Collection République des idées, Paris: Seuil.

Béchard, Jean-Pierre (1994), 'Les grandes questions de recherche en entrepreneurship et education', Cahier de Recherche No. 94-11-02, Montreal: HEC Montréal.

Beranger, Jacques, Robert Chabbal and Fabrice Dambrine (1998), 'Rapport sur la formation des ingénieurs à l'entrepreneuriat' (Report on entrepreneurial training of engineers). Report to the Secretary of State in charge of Industry.

Bosma, N.S., Z.J. Acs, E. Autio, A. Coduras and J. Levie (2009), 'Global Entrepreneurship Monitor 2008', Executive Report, Babson College/Universidad del Desarollo/Global Entrepreneurship Research Association, downloadable at www.gemconsortium.org.

Carayannis, E.G., D. Evans and M. Hanson (2003), 'A cross-cultural learning strategy for entrepreneurship education: outline of key concepts and lessons learned from a comparative study of entrepreneurship students in France and the US', *Technovation*, **23** (9): 757–71.

European Commission (2008), 'Survey of entrepreneurship in higher education in Europe', NIRAS Consultants, FORA, ECON Pöyry Survey of Entrepreneurship Education in Higher Education in Europe.

Fayolle, Alain (1997), 'L'enseignement de l'entrepreneuriat : réflexions autour d'une expérience', Ecole de Management de Lyon, Ecully, France.

Fayolle, Alain (1999), 'L'enseignement de l'entrepreneuriat dans les universités françaises: analyse de l'existant et propositions pour en faciliter le développement', Ecole de Management de Lyon, Ecully, France.

Fendt, J. and S. Bureau (2010), 'Small business education in a *grande nation*: antinomy, opportunity or both? A French *grande école* case study', in Alain Fayolle (ed.), *Handbook of Research in Entrepreneurship Education, Volume 3: International Perspectives*, Cheltenham, UK and Northampton, MA, USA: Edward Elgar, pp. 86–109.

Financial Times (2009), 'European Business School rankings 2009', available at: http://rankings.ft.com/businessschoolrankings/european-business-school-rankings.

Henriquez, Candice, Ingrid Verheul, Ineke van der Knaap and Casandra Bischoff (2001), 'Determinants of entrepreneurship in France: policies, institutions and culture', Institute for Development Strategies, Indiana University. Available from http://www.spea.indiana.edu/ids/pdfholder/ISSN-01-4.pdf.

INSEE (2009), 'Créations et défaillances d'entreprises', Paris: INSEE.

Klapper, Rita (2004), 'Government goals and entrepreneurship education: an investigation at a grande école in France', *Education + Training*, **46** (3): 127–37.

Léger-Jarniou, Catherine (2001), 'La création d'entreprise par les jeunes: mythes ou réalités?', Actes du Séminaire INSEE, Création d'entreprise, projets et réalisations, Paris: INSEE.

OECD (2007), *Enhancing Incentives to Improve Performance in the Education System*, OECD Economic Surveys, Paris: OECD.

Torres, O. and A. Eminet (2005), 'L'entrepreneuriat en France et dans le monde', French Executive Report, Global Entrepreneurship Monitor.

Veltz, P. (2007), *Faut-il sauver les Grandes Ecoles? De la culture de la sélection à la culture de l'innovation*, Paris: Presses de Sciences Politiques.

4.   University of Southern California

Kathleen Allen and Mark Lieberman

The entrepreneurship ecosystem at the University of Southern California (USC) began in the 1960s when the university offered its first courses dedicated to helping students understand the mindset and skills required to launch new businesses. The elaborate innovation and entrepreneurship ecosystem that exists at USC today was not the result of a decades-long strategy to develop such an ecosystem. Rather it emerged organically in much the same way as the field of entrepreneurship, pushed by a growing demand from students, researchers and the community for a unified system of resources and expertise that they could tap into as they developed their businesses or commercialized their research.

This chapter explores the nature and evolution of the USC entrepreneurship ecosystem. The chapter is organized according to a modified framework proposed by Hansen and Birkinshaw (2007) that describes the innovation value chain. It consists of three broad phases: idea generation, conversion and diffusion. Within each phase are activities that involve collaboration, screening and developing, and spreading ideas within and outside the organization. Reflecting the three phases, the chapter comprises three parts: (1) the genesis of an entrepreneurship ecosystem; (2) the development of the innovation and entrepreneurship ecosystem; and (3) the diffusion of the entrepreneurial mindset and skills within and outside the university.

THE GENESIS OF AN ENTREPRENEURSHIP ECOSYSTEM

To appreciate why the study of entrepreneurship developed so early at USC, it is important to understand the context in which the university operates. USC is located in downtown Los Angeles at the center of a highly diverse metropolitan area that is part of the greater Southern California region extending from Santa Barbara in the north to San Diego in the south. Los Angeles County alone accounts for $442 billion in annual output and its population exceeds 10 million.

USC was founded in 1880. Today it is home to over 33 000 students and nearly 3200 full-time faculty members on one of the most ethnically diverse campuses in the United States. USC is among the top 20 research universities in the United States, bringing in well over $500 million in annual research funding. Other significant research universities that have entrepreneurship courses or programs are located in Southern California: UCLA, Caltech, UC Irvine, and UC San Diego. The 20 largest schools in Southern California support over 400 000 students (Education Portal 2010). More than 200 colleges and universities are located in Southern California, making it a center for education and research. In addition, the Los Angeles region supports the largest angel network in the United States, the Tech Coast Angels, as well as several smaller angel networks.

The diversity of the region is reflected in its various technology clusters that include aerospace, media and entertainment, port technologies, biotechnology, intermodal transportation, green technologies, and engineering and medical devices. Technology-led entrepreneurship is influenced by these clusters and is supported by an educated workforce and easy access to global transport.

The entrepreneurship ecosystem at the University of Southern California began its evolution in the 1960s when the first courses in entrepreneurship were offered. Entrepreneurship as an academic subject was unusual at the time because this was a period of relative stability in the United States when gigantic companies experienced little competition from Europe and offered lifetime job security for their employees. There was little incentive to start small companies. Nevertheless courses in entrepreneurship were received with great enthusiasm by students who wanted to blaze a new trail in the business world. By 1971 demand for courses warranted the development of a graduate program in entrepreneurship with an advisory board of entrepreneur alumni and professional service providers. At the same time, USC established the Office of Technology Licensing (OTL) to address the needs of researchers who wanted to commercialize the results of their research largely through licensing to large companies. The OTL had three primary goals:

1. to transfer intellectual property (IP) developed at USC;
2. to protect IP developed at USC;
3. to ensure compliance with federal statutes, regulations and reporting requirements.

The OTL transferred IP developed at USC to industry for the betterment of society and to increase university revenues by licensing patents and copyrights. Various forms of licensing agreements were developed by USC's Office of the General Counsel, which reviewed each agreement and sent it for approval by the Office of the Senior Vice President for Administration. A key component of OTL's process was protecting USC's IP through the prosecution and maintenance of patents, the registration of copyrights and other activities. Outside attorneys were retained for these functions. OTL was also responsible for the federal reporting requirements that are part of the university's obligations to US government agencies and other research sponsors.

During this period, the OTL was largely focused on licensing to industry, so no real connections were established with the Greif Entrepreneurship Center, which is the primary focal point for entrepreneurship at USC. This is not surprising given that the Bayh–Dole Act, which gave universities the right to own and commercialize government-funded research, did not take effect until 1986. It would still be a number of years before the entrepreneurial link was made to scientific and engineering research.

DEVELOPING THE INNOVATION AND ENTREPRENEURSHIP ECOSYSTEM

Box 4.1 is a chronology of significant events in the development of the innovation and entrepreneurship ecosystem at USC after the seeds were planted in the mid to late 1960s.

The launch of the graduate entrepreneurship program in 1971 was followed in 1980 by the start of a renowned undergraduate program in entrepreneurship. The 1980s are often referred to as the decade of entrepreneurship (Case 1992). Big business was suffering the effects of new regulations, increasing foreign competition and the technological revolution that rendered whole categories of products obsolete. The economic focus was now on smaller, more flexible companies, and this trend spurred an increased interest in entrepreneurship. During their senior year at USC, 150 undergraduates entered the entrepreneurship program after a competitive application process and took four mandatory courses that required them to create two business plans, one as a team and one as individuals. Between the 1971 launch of this program and 2000, an average of 37 percent of the students annually launched businesses by the time they graduated, reflecting the sharply increasing interest in entrepreneurship as an area of study and the business climate that supported entrepreneurial ventures.

In spring 1996, the Entrepreneur Program, which up to this point had been focused at the Marshall School of Business, began offering the first undergraduate course at the Marshall School designed to serve the needs of engineering students who wanted to substitute an entrepreneurship

BOX 4.1   IMPORTANT EVENTS IN THE
DEVELOPMENT OF USC
ENTREPRENEURSHIP ECOSYSTEM

1960s	First courses offered in entrepreneurship at the gradu-ate level
1971	First undergraduate course
1971	Establishment of the Office of Technology Licensing
1971	Concentration in entrepreneurship at the MBA level
1980	Concentration in entrepreneurship at the undergraduate level
1997	Lloyd Greif endowment of entrepreneurship center
1998	Founding of Technology Commercialization Alliance
2004	Founding of USC Marshall Center for Technology Commercialization
2004	Certificate in Technology Commercialization
2005	Entrepreneurship becomes a required course in MBA-PM
2007	Founding of USC Stevens Institute for Innovation as the new home of the Office of Technology Licensing

course for the required engineering economics. This was the first time that a business course had been approved as part of a degree program in electrical engineering and computer science.

The Entrepreneur Program achieved a significant milestone in 1997 when alumnus Lloyd Greif, who had founded a boutique investment banking firm in Los Angeles, Greif & Co., endowed the program with $5 million, the first such endowment from an alumnus in the United States. This endowment gave the program an annual operating budget, which enabled a number of new programs and events to be funded. The center became the Lloyd Greif Center for Entrepreneurial Studies, and the endowment agreement stated that the Lloyd Greif Center owned the exclusive rights to the term 'entrepreneurship' in titles of courses and programs at the university. The year 1997 was just the beginning of what would become the dotcom bubble. Interest in entrepreneurship skyrocketed across campus. At the time when the endowment agreement was secured, no one could have predicted how often another entity on campus would want to use the term 'entrepreneur' or 'entrepreneurship' in the title of a course or event. Each time the infringing entity was asked to change its name so that it did not include the words 'entrepreneur' or 'entrepreneurship'. This strategy to protect the brand was due in large part to Lloyd Greif's active involvement in the center in terms of influencing strategic direction and policy.

The ecosystem at this point was relatively small and centered on business entrepreneurship. Entrepreneurship activities were occurring on an ad hoc basis in other parts of campus, for example the School of Engineering, but there was no coordinated effort to identify and optimize resources to support entrepreneurs. Engineers, scientists and others were becoming increasingly aware of the commercial potential of their research largely due to stories in the press about entrepreneurs completing initial public offerings (IPOs) or raising venture financing for previously unheard of amounts of money. These researchers began seeking guidance from USC faculty and alumni who had successfully launched ventures. Some of the researchers found their way to the Greif Center, most likely because of the awareness created by the press surrounding the endowment.

In October 1998 the Greif Center was contacted by Martin Gunderson, the Chair of the Electrophysics Department in the School of Engineering, who had read about the technology commercialization work being done in the Greif Center in the *LA Times*. The Chair wanted to create awareness for the School of Engineering's new technology initiative and the institute that had been created through a $100 million endowment from the entrepreneur Alfred Mann. He wanted to collaborate with the Greif Center in those efforts. That initial contact precipitated a six-year effort on the part of Kathleen Allen (Marshall School of Business), George Bekey (Viterbi School of Engineering) and others to establish what was recognized by the university and the deans of the schools of business, engineering, and medicine as the USC Technology Commercialization Alliance (TCA). What started as a collaboration to discover mutual interests grew to include the College of Letters, Arts, and Sciences and the School of Pharmacy, and it became the central source of information, research, education and services related to the commercialization of USC technology through entrepreneurship for faculty, researchers and students.

TCA assisted inventors with market feasibility analysis, business plan development, start-up financing, management team acquisition and related issues. More specifically, TCA's objectives were:

1. to promote the transfer of research advances and new technologies into goods and services available to the general public;
2. to maximize financial return on the university's portfolio of intellectual property;
3. to attract and retain students, staff and faculty with entrepreneurial interests and talent and serve as an applied research center;

4. to provide opportunities for students to apply knowledge acquired in the classroom to a real-world business environment and potentially become stakeholders in start-up ventures.

In 2004 the TCA became the USC Marshall Center for Technology Commercialization (CTC). It expanded its offerings to work with existing USC commercialization entities and the Greif Entrepreneurship Center to provide referrals, information, education, advice, assistance and services on all aspects of technology commercialization for USC faculty, staff and student researchers. CTC provided these services and resources in person, by referrals to other on-campus organizations and via the CTC website. The CTC Advisory Board consisted of active members of the technology community including angel investors, attorneys, entrepreneurs and senior executives from large technology-related firms. The board members played an active role in both policy and mentoring.

Introduction to New Ventures became a required course in the Marshall MBA Program for Professionals and Managers (MBA.PM) in 2005. It was the first required course in entrepreneurship at USC. At about the same time, an entrepreneurship module was introduced to the full-time MBA core program, which meant that the discipline of entrepreneurship now touched all Marshall MBA students.

In 2007 the Office of Technology Licensing became part of the new USC Stevens Institute for Innovation, endowed by venture capitalist Mark Stevens of Sequoia Capital, in an effort to streamline its services and more effectively transfer the results of research to society in the form of new products and services. To perform these functions, the OTL office was organized into marketing teams, with a broad-based support and administration team. Each marketing team, organized by specialty and technical area, comprises a technology licensing associate (TLA) and a marketing assistant and is responsible for effectively marketing and licensing technologies from particular academic areas of the university. A separate office is located on the Health Sciences Campus to meet the needs of that community better.

Today the entrepreneurship ecosystem at the University of Southern California is led by three primary nodes of activity: (1) the Lloyd Greif Center for Entrepreneurial Studies, which is the home for entrepreneurship education on the campus; (2) the USC Marshall Center for Technology Commercialization, which developed out of the original Technology Commercialization Alliance as a spin-off of the Greif Center to focus on the unique needs of researchers, faculty and students who are developing new technologies with market applications; and (3) the USC Stevens Institute for Innovation, which is responsible for managing intellectual property through its Office of Technology Licensing and for facilitating programs that encourage innovation on both campuses.

Faculty and Staff

The Greif Entrepreneurship Center maintains a full-time director in a faculty position, eight full-time and four adjunct, or part-time, faculty members. Faculty are assigned exclusively to the Greif Center and they hold clinical faculty positions in the Marshall School of Business. Clinical faculty have all the rights and promotion benefits of tenure-track faculty, but their primary focus is teaching. In 2009 the Greif Center had three full professors, one associate professor and four assistant professors in full-time positions. In addition, the center employs two full-time staff and several student workers.

Full-time faculty teach a four- to six-course load annually; they are evaluated on teaching, service and, in some cases, research. Many courses are team taught, especially those that form the foundational curriculum. The director of the USC Marshall Center for Technology Commercialization (CTC) is also a faculty member in the Greif Center and shares staff with the Greif Center. The Center for Ethics and Social Responsibility focuses on entrepreneurial ventures that have a triple bottom line objective. (Triple bottom line means using ecological and social criteria for measuring organizational success, in addition to financial performance.) Its director also holds a faculty position in the management department. The full-time executive director of the USC Stevens Institute for Innovation is also the vice-provost of the university, overseeing 25 staff positions including technology licensing officers.

Faculty members are encouraged to become experts in niche areas of entrepreneurship such as technology commercialization, venture capital, acquiring businesses and entrepreneurial marketing. They also receive support to participate in entrepreneurship-focused conferences with no limit on the number of conferences they can attend. New faculty members typically teach with senior faculty the first time they teach one of the core entrepreneurship courses.

Teaching and Learning

The Greif Center maintains a diverse course offering that is limited only by the Marshall School requirements on the minimum number of students per class, which currently stands at 35. Table 4.1 presents the curriculum at the graduate and undergraduate levels within the Greif Entrepreneurship Center.

Table 4.1   Greif Center curriculum

Graduate courses	Undergraduate courses
BAEP 551 Introduction to New Ventures	BAEP 301 Entrepreneurship for Engineers
BAEP 552 Cases in Entrepreneurship: Feasibility Analysis	BAEP 451 Introduction to New Ventures
BAEP 553 CEO/Founder Cases in New Venture Management	BAEP 452 Cases in Entrepreneurship: Feasibility Analysis
BAEP 554 Business Plan	BAEP 453 Venture Management
BAEP 555 Management of Rapidly Growing Ventures	BAEP 454 Business Plan
BAEP 556 Technology Feasibility	BUAD 301 Technical Entrepreneurship
BAEP 557 Technology Commercialization	
BAEP 558 Acquiring a Business	
BAEP 559 Investing in New Ventures	

Entrepreneurship Majors, Minors and Emphases

At the graduate level, students can complete an emphasis in entrepreneurship that prepares them to enter the business world with an entrepreneurial mindset and the skills required to recognize opportunity, develop a business concept, test that concept through a feasibility analysis and write a comprehensive business plan. That emphasis requires taking Introduction to New Ventures, Feasibility Analysis, Business Plan and one other course of the student's choosing.

At the undergraduate level, students can complete a senior option in entrepreneurship or experiment with one or more courses. Similar to the graduate program, the undergraduate program takes an applied approach, preparing students to deal effectively in the business world while taking advantage of an entrepreneurial mindset and the skills to recognize opportunity, develop business concepts, test those concepts and complete a business plan. The senior option consists of courses in Introduction to New Ventures, Feasibility Analysis, Starting and Growing the Business, and Business Plan.

Undergraduates can also take a minor in entrepreneurship that consists of sixteen units. The three required courses are Management of New Enterprises or Technical Entrepreneurship, Cases in Entrepreneurship, and Management of Small Businesses. They chose one additional course from several offered.

Entrepreneurship Electives

All courses in entrepreneurship at USC are considered electives with the exception of the pre-fall intensive course offered in the MBA.PM program during a weekend in August before the second year. The purpose of the intensive, which lasts two and a half days, is to provide students with an overview of entrepreneurship concepts so that they can take the feasibility course in the fall semester. The full-time MBAs must take Introduction to New Ventures as a prerequisite to feasibility analysis.

RSCI 601: Biomedical Commerce
In collaboration with the Regulatory Science Program at the USC School zof Pharmacy, a mini-course in opportunity recognition with an overview of feasibility analysis and business plan construction was developed. The purpose is to help science students see the business side of the life science industries.

Certificate in Technology Commercialization
The Certificate in Technology Commercialization (see Table 4.2) provides students with a variety of opportunities to gain knowledge and develop skills related to commercialization. The student learning experience – part academic and part real world – includes theory and practice. Students participate in a living laboratory program to experience the entire spectrum of the commercialization process – invention, product development, technical and market feasibility analysis, intellectual property acquisition,

Table 4.2   Certificate in Technology Commercialization

Required courses	Elective courses (students choose one)
BAEP 557 Technology Commercialization	BAEP 553 Cases in New Venture Management
BAEP 556 Technology Feasibility	BAEP 555 Management of Rapidly Growing Ventures
BAEP 559 Investing in New Ventures	MOR 561 Strategies in High-Tech Businesses
	ISE 585 Strategic Management of Technology
	ISE 555 Invention and Technology Development
	ISE 515 Engineering Project Management

business planning and venture funding – while potentially becoming stakeholders in a new technology venture. They are also eligible to apply for summer internships sponsored by industry partners to give them additional experience in taking a new technology to market.

The program is particularly suited to those in science, engineering and business. Classes are made up of masters- and PhD-level researchers in medicine, the sciences and all areas of engineering as well as MBA candidates. The completed certificate is awarded by USC and is documented on the graduate's transcript.

BAEP 453: Venture management

This new undergraduate class successfully debuted in 2009. It concentrates on classroom and practical studies with an emphasis on customer research and testing, customer acquisition, networking and presentation skills. The classroom work is followed by a lab that illustrates a real-life situation. Each student or team of students is presented with four challenges or projects. The first challenge is to identify a market pain that has the potential for a practical solution. The next three challenges involve putting the concept into action, a guerilla marketing task and a philanthropy task. By the end of the class, students will have tested a real business concept both in the class and in the real world.

Research

The research mission of the Greif Center is to develop, support and disseminate leading-edge interdisciplinary scholarship in entrepreneurship. This scholarship should meet the highest standards of scientific rigor and examine questions and problems that are central to the practice of entrepreneurship. The Greif Center has no tenure-track positions assigned to it, so it maintains an extensive network of affiliated research faculty and doctoral students from across the Marshall School and USC to promote interdisciplinary research in entrepreneurship. To achieve the research mission, the Greif Center organizes and supports a wide range of research-related activities. These activities are displayed in Table 4.3.

DIFFUSING THE ENTREPRENEURIAL MINDSET WITHIN AND OUTSIDE THE UNIVERSITY

In this section, the focus is on how the entrepreneurship activities of the primary nodes in the entrepreneurship ecosystem are spread throughout

Table 4.3   Greif Center research activities

Activity	Purpose
Greif Seminar Series	Brings leading entrepreneurship researchers to Marshall School to present recent work
Greif Conferences	Unites academics from around the world to present and discuss recent research
Greif Research Impact Award	Annual $5000 award given to the researcher(s) who published the most impactful entrepreneurship article six years ago in top management and entrepreneurship journals; database tracks publication and citation of entrepreneurship articles
Greif Faculty Research Award	Offers research support to faculty members for entrepreneurship-related projects through an annual $5000 award
Greif Doctoral Student Research Award	Annual $2500 scholarship for a USC doctoral student for research in entrepreneurship
Visiting Researcher Program	Greif Center welcomes researchers from around the globe to visit Marshall and conduct research in the Los Angeles area; recent researchers have come from New Zealand, Belgium and China

the internal and external community. Figure 4.1 displays the key nodes of the entrepreneurship ecosystem at USC.

Faculty-Led Outreach Activities

The faculty of the Greif Center is active in promoting entrepreneurship on and off campus through a variety of events and activities. Some of the more prominent activities are discussed here. Faculty members also spend an extraordinary amount of time mentoring and guiding entrepreneurs on campus and in the community.

New venture competition
Formerly called the Business Plan Competition, the New Venture Competition (NVC) recognizes achievement in developing a new business and realizing a proof of the concept. Faculty, staff and students from both USC campuses can enter the competition. For many years the Greif Center resisted the idea of a business plan competition because observation of many competitions around the country led to the conclusion that the competition was more about the plan than about the actual business

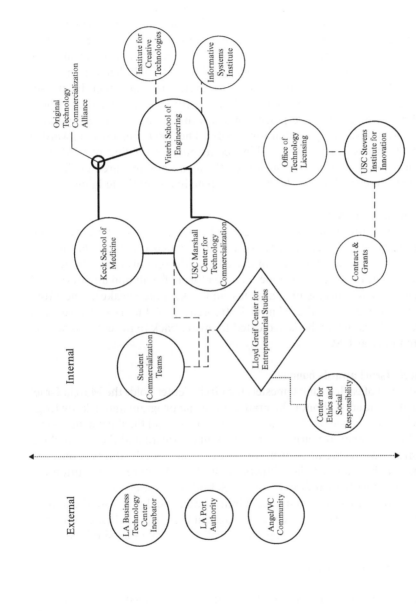

Figure 4.1 University of Southern California entrepreneurship ecosystem

being presented. The goal was to celebrate new businesses that would actually be launched within six months of receiving a prize. The Greif Center held its first competition in 2004. Since that time, only one business that won a prize has not become a revenue-generating company.

Applicants submit a five-page executive summary and exhibits and are judged in two rounds. In the first round, a panel of angel investors examines the documents submitted and determines which applicants have presented a compelling case for their business and will therefore move to the final round. In the final round, six to seven teams pitch their businesses before a panel of judges composed of entrepreneurs, venture capitalists and angel investors. The judges choose winners in various competition categories based on potential for success. The 2009 competition awarded $60000 in cash prizes plus in-kind contributions totaling over $10000. Faculty in the Greif Center mentored the teams and prepared the finalists for their pitches. Faculty did not participate in any of the judging.

Alumni network day
The first Saturday of March is dedicated to the alumni of the Lloyd Greif Entrepreneurship Center. This is a well-attended event for 300 to 400 individuals who want to stay connected with the school and celebrate their success. The day usually includes an open forum for alumni updates, panel discussions by successful graduates and a keynote speaker. The Greif Center also bestows the Alumni Entrepreneur of the Year award on a successful graduate who is dedicated to giving back to the entrepreneurial community at USC.

Marcia Israel awards banquet
At the end of each spring semester, the Greif Center holds the Marcia Israel awards banquet to honor the graduates of the program and acknowledge special achievements. The honors include the Pound the Pavement award, the Entrepreneurial Spirit Award, the Values Award and the Networking Award. Awards are also given for best feasibility study and best business plan. At this banquet the winners of the New Venture Competition are announced with great fanfare and a celebratory large check.

In addition to these activities, Greif Center faculty choose the annual Entrepreneur of the Year, serve as judges in the Hispanic Entrepreneur of the Year national awards program as well as several other similar events.

University-Led Activities

The USC Stevens Institute for Innovation was founded in 2007 with the goal of fostering innovation throughout both campuses. It reports directly to the provost and is also charged with managing the disclosure, patent and licensing functions of the university. To that end it has increased its IP and licensing staff to 25 with plans to grow to 32. The Institute holds a number of important events and programs, including the Global Impact program that sends students to India for the summer to find solutions to problems identified by their collaborators in India; Matchyard, a Facebook application that connects innovators with resources; TEDxUSC, the first university-hosted TED (Technology, Entertainment, Design) conference; the Innovation Leadership Council, a student-run organization that stimulates innovation throughout the university; and a number of networking events.

Student-Led Activities

Students at USC develop and run activities as part of the entrepreneurship ecosystem. The Entrepreneur and Venture Management Association (EVMA) is a graduate organization whose mission is to support students interested in 'pursuing dynamic, growth-oriented career opportunities'. The club offers access to networking events, venture capitalists and a speaker series. It also hosts two forums: an entrepreneur roundtable, where those ready to launch new ventures can talk to their peers; and a venture capital roundtable.

The EVMA also runs the Venture Capital Investment Challenge. The challenge exposes students to the venture capital experience. Students play the role of venture capitalist and participate in real-world pitches. Local venture capitalists observe and judge the students on their evaluations and analysis of the pitches. Student teams present their recommendations to the local venture capitalists in a round-robin format.

The Entrepreneur Club (eClub) is the largest student club on campus. The eClub is for undergraduates who are considering starting or buying a business. The club offers networking events and a speaker series that includes successful entrepreneurs, topic experts, investors and others. A monthly newsletter and web page keep the members of this club updated. A number of other niche-specific organizations have sprung up to serve particular interests. They often combine forces to produce events and help each other achieve their goals.

Alumni Activities

A large part of the USC ecosystem is the alumni, a network for which USC is well known. One of the most important attributes of the alumni is their willingness to give back to the university with money, jobs, internships and time. The alumni have formalized a number of organizations. The Trojan CEO Network is an exclusive, invitation-only organization for USC alumni CEOs. This network is similar to other peer-to-peer organizations like Young Presidents' Organization (YPO) and Vistage (formerly TEC). Its goals are to share knowledge and experiences and to continue learning and building skill sets. The network is open only to USC alumni who are CEOs of early-stage organizations. It is anticipated that this network will fill the void until the CEOs' organization reaches a revenue stage that permits the members to join their local YPO chapter. In 2009 there were 40 members of this new organization with six subgroups, including a virtual group that meets online. Approximately once a quarter the entire network gathers for an educational event that is tied to another event on campus.

The Marshall Alumni Association maintains five chapters with a very active leadership. They have a dedicated website within the Marshall School of Business and a healthy calendar of events year round. They are also linked to the 100 other general and individual USC alumni associations. These include the USC Alumni Association and the numerous guilds and leagues that support the university. Membership in the Marshall Alumni Association offers a number of benefits that include invitations to school, university and alumni-sponsored family events; roundtable discussions with industry leaders, the dean and faculty; newsletters; campus tours and introductions; access to the Marshall network of 70 000 alumni; library access; and invitations to USC football picnics.

Community Outreach

A university does not exist in isolation. Creating and retaining relationships with the community outside of regular university life is a key factor in the success of many programs. There are a number of connections to the community, but relationships based upon mutual benefit are the glue that cements and fosters these activities. Several of these programs are part of the entrepreneurship ecosystem at USC.

One notable program is the Los Angeles Community Impact (LACI) program for undergraduate business students. LACI assists non-profits and small businesses in Los Angeles with business-related challenges. Each LACI consulting team is paired with a university professor as a mentor to complete a well-researched, implementable plan. Another organization that has been close to the Greif Center is the National Foundation for Teaching Entrepreneurship (NFTE). NFTE works with inner-city youth to teach the basics of entrepreneurship and small business. Faculty have mentored students, worked as judges in their competitions and hosted their regional finals.

Angel and venture community
The Tech Coast Angels is the largest angel investment group in the United States. They are local to Southern California and have over 300 members. Other angel groups include the Pasadena Angels and the Maverick Angels. All of the investor groups are active at the university as mentors to start-ups that are evolving out of the Greif Center and the Center for Technology Commercialization and as judges at various pitch competitions. The Tech Coast Angels regularly hold deal-screening sessions on campus that a limited number of students are allowed to attend. The students are afforded the rare opportunity to see the behind-the-scenes discussions after each pitch session and to develop a better understanding of investment decision making. Students report that this is one of the highlights of the semester. The angel groups have intern programs that enable students to work with the members on due-diligence issues or in portfolio companies. In addition, the angels often hire graduating students to work as administrators for their organization. This position is extremely important to the angels because the administrator is first point of contact for entrepreneurs and is the first screener for new deals.

Incubators
The university has active participation from one of the largest technology incubators in the country, the Business Technology Center (BTC) of Los Angeles County. The BTC is a project of the Community Development Commission of Los Angeles County. Government support of an incubator is important to the vitality of the regional entrepreneurship ecosystem. Technology start-ups have easy access to a host of opportunities surrounding the technology community in Los Angeles. The BTC also runs Los Angeles County Technology Week in which USC participates. The week-long series of events has become a showcase for innovation in the region. Entrepreneurs from the incubator are often guest speakers in classes, and they sometimes hire students as part-time interns. A number of students have also found permanent positions among incubator clients. Many technology start-ups from the university have gravitated to the BTC for guidance during the critical launch stage. In addition, Los Angeles County is planning another incubator to be located next to the university's medical center. The BTC has an established international beachhead program that provides additional opportunities for student entrepreneurs. The BTC enjoys agreements with Japan, Korea and New Zealand, and with Australia in Victoria and Western Australia.

Port of Los Angeles
The Marshall Center for Technology Commercialization has recently signed a memorandum of understanding with the Port of Los Angeles to support its new incubator program. When launched, CTC will assist with technology feasibility studies, interns and access to new research and collaboration.

SUMMARY OF LESSONS LEARNED

All the lessons learned about creating and growing an entrepreneurship ecosystem can be distilled into two words: 'people' and 'patience'. Jim Collins hit the nail on the head when he wrote in *Good to Great* about the importance of getting the right people on the bus and in the right seats (Collins 2001). Unlike many other institutions and programs that universities build, an entrepreneurship ecosystem is typically organic, starting at a grass-roots level with small efforts throughout the university that receive little attention. As these smaller efforts combine to address larger problems, they are eventually pulled together into a collaborative network.

At USC attempts to own innovation or entrepreneurship in specific institutes or centers have largely failed because innovation and entrepreneurship are activities that do not respond well to formal processes but rather bubble up in many diverse ways. However a vision at the highest levels that supports innovation and entrepreneurship and considers it critical to the mission of the university is essential to the successful development of an ecosystem. At USC, President Sample's leadership and vision for the university have always included these elements, and they are also reflected in the number of entrepreneurs on the board of trustees.

That has not always been the case at the level of the business school dean. Since 2000 the Marshall School has gone through four deans (one was an interim appointment). Each one stated that entrepreneurship was important and each one recognized that a great many students come to the Marshall School specifically for entrepreneurship. Nevertheless the reality is that business schools are generally ranked based on what recruiters say and what the full-time MBAs report about their school. Because entrepreneurship as a discipline does not directly affect the rankings of a business school, it does not receive the same respect as core disciplines like finance, management and marketing. This bias holds true in research as well. No entrepreneurship journals are rated in the top five academic journals according to the Marshall School; they are considered second-tier journals for purposes of evaluating publications for tenure. Yet Marshall deans have always acknowledged the importance of entrepreneurship to their role in the university. It could be argued that the primary job of a dean is fund-raising, and at USC, like other universities, the bulk of the endowments, scholarships and buildings come from successful entrepreneurs such as Gordon Marshall (Marshall Industries), Andrew Viterbi (Qualcom), Alfred Mann (Advanced Bionics, Second Sight) and Paul Orfalea (Kinkos).

The real work of creating the entrepreneurship ecosystem at USC has occurred within departments and laboratories and among the various student organizations. Organic, grass-roots-level growth of this type is slow and often blocked by challenges that can impede or halt progress. The structural organization of the university into profit centers, for example, makes the cross-disciplinary collaboration needed for an effective ecosystem difficult at best. Concerns about sharing tuition revenues, faculty salaries and general expenses often create barriers that are difficult to overcome. Endowment agreements can stifle the rapid growth of the ecosystem, especially when an endowed center is further challenged by the inertia of success, which makes continued growth difficult.

As discussed previously, at USC, the term 'entrepreneurship' is owned by the Lloyd Greif Center for Entrepreneurial Studies, which is consistently ranked among the top entrepreneurship centers in the United States. This clause in the endowment contract has not halted entrepreneurial efforts in the rest of the university, but rather it has forced other entities to think creatively about how to deliver their message. They have generally resorted to developing inventive terminology to describe their entrepreneurial efforts. For example the Regulatory Science Program uses the expression 'biomedical commerce', USC Stevens has become the USC Stevens Institute for Innovation, and the Viterbi School of Engineering uses the word 'enterprise' for many of its entrepreneurship activities. Because entrepreneurship is a topic of universal interest and receives so much attention in the press, it is impossible to corral it into one area of the university. The fact that entrepreneurship is cropping up across all parts of the university is a testament to its power and to the determination of those who are pursuing new entrepreneurship efforts despite the challenges they face.

Student organizations are another example of grass-roots entrepreneurship efforts. The Entrepreneur Club at the undergraduate level and the Entrepreneurial Venture Management Association at the graduate level are the largest clubs at USC. Both are supported by the Greif Entrepreneurship Center.

It has recently become clear that the new generation of students – the Millennials – are bringing fresh challenges to the ecosystem in terms of academic programs and other structured activities. Their learning style and social values are quite distinct from those of the generation that preceded them. Entrepreneurship has been part of their lexicon for their entire lives and the Internet has played a critical role in the kinds of businesses to which they tend to gravitate. At the same time, this generation of students understands the importance of collaboration and the power of social networks so there is hope that the ecosystem can advance even more rapidly as more of these students become involved.

Champions and relationships are key elements in the success of any ecosystem. Finding like-minded individuals in the various schools and organizations on the USC campus was critical in driving the collaborations that support a thriving ecosystem and in identifying ways to ensure mutual benefit. Champions have emerged in rather opportunistic and altruistic ways despite a lack of incentives or rewards. A champion or key individual most often takes responsibility for each major node of the ecosystem, but even after years of evolution, there is no formal structure for bringing together all the nodes of the ecosystem to coordinate efforts. As a result there is still some overlap in activities, and the current ecosystem is probably not operating as efficiently as it could be. The champions hold the larger strategic vision for the ecosystem, but have difficulty implementing that vision in a bureaucratic university system that wants this type of cross-disciplinary activity but bestows rewards on the basis of where tuition and research dollars are housed. This can create conflict because the very nature of entrepreneurship – dynamic, uncertain, ambiguous – does not readily lend itself to a great deal of structure. People seem to connect when they need to and share information through the usual channels of email, websites and newsletters.

In terms of the relationships between the university nodes and the community and region, the primary areas of connection and collaboration are with alumni entrepreneurs, the LA Business Technology Center, local industries that support innovation at the university such as the private space industry, the LA Port Authority, and the angel and venture capital community. These collaborations take the form of lecturing in classes, mentoring entrepreneurship teams, conducting feasibility analyses for alumni entrepreneurs, providing internships in companies and funding specific innovation projects. The Los Angeles region contains a multitude of organizations that are also focused on supporting entrepreneurs, so the need for the university to be directly involved in economic development is not as great as it may be for universities that are the primary higher education institution in a region.

This chapter describes the creation and evolution of the innovation and entrepreneurship ecosystem at the University of Southern California. We believe that our experience contains many lessons for those who want to develop such an ecosystem. There is no one best way to create an entrepreneurship ecosystem. In our experience, it is a multistage process where the stages are not clearly defined as the university moves through them. Each stage develops relationships and capabilities that enable the ecosystem to evolve to the next level. An entrepreneurship ecosystem is a living, breathing, amorphous being that changes with the times and the people who are part of it. Finding ways to encourage the natural growth of the ecosystem without the constraints of an onerous bureaucracy will ensure that the entrepreneurial mindset and the positive outcomes of entrepreneurship activities are facilitated and encouraged to grow.

REFERENCES

Case, John (1992), *From the Ground Up: The Resurgence of American Entrepreneurship*, New York: Simon & Schuster.

Collins, Jim (2001), *Good to Great*, New York: Collins Business.

Education Portal (2010), 'Southern California colleges and universities: what are the largest Southern California colleges and universities?', Education-Portal.com, available at: http://education-portal.com/southern_california_colleges_and_universities.html (accessed 31 March 2010).

Hansen, M.T. and J. Birkinshaw (2007), 'The innovation value chain', *Harvard Business Review*, Reprint R0706J.

PART II

Entrepreneurship Ecosystems: Technology Transfer and Commercialization

5. The University of Texas at Austin

John Sibley Butler

Entrepreneurship, along with science and technology, is altering our society domestically and globally. The solutions to many critical issues and problems now demand an integrated, holistic flexible approach that blends technology, management, and scientific, socio-economic, cultural and political ramifications in an atmosphere of profound change and extreme compression.

(George Kozmetsky 1993)

Innovation and entrepreneurship stand at the very center of job creation and wealth creation within market economies. The last three decades, since the 1980s, have seen the emergence of high-tech communities along with a corresponding development of a strong body of academic research targeted towards explaining how these communities actually evolved. In this literature Silicon Valley, Austin, Texas and Route 128 in Boston are the most frequently investigated sites for case studies (Smilor et al. 1998). Central to this research agenda is the concept of the business ecosystem. The purpose of this chapter is to: (1) trace the theoretical modeling and history of business ecosystems; (2) examine how these models enrich our understanding of such ecosystems; and (3) show how the methodology of the IC² Institute at The University of Texas at Austin enhanced the ecosystem for that region.

THEORETICAL CONSIDERATIONS

Diffusion Theory

To understand the development of high-tech communities, we must start with the theory of the diffusion of innovation. Diffusion scholars are concerned with the process by which an innovation, whether an idea, a process or a technology, is communicated through channels over time among members of a social system. In this consideration the social system is a business community concerned with entrepreneurship and technology transfer as a means of job and wealth creation. Diffusion scholarship allows us to understand the development and commercialization of technologies as companies are created; it also helps us to understand the importance of the actors who champion change as communities are transformed into high-tech centers. Finally it helps us to model why certain communities become rich with business ecosystems while others do not.

Diffusion theory can be traced to the work of Gabriel Tarde, a scholar of sociology and psychology who was interested in why, 'given hundreds of innovations conceived at the same time – innovations in the form of words, in mythological ideas, in industrial processes, etc. – ten will spread abroad while ninety will be forgotten' (Tarde 1903, 140). He posited the adoption or rejection of innovations as a major research question. As early as 1903 he hypothesized that the rate of adoption of new innovations assumed an s-shaped curve when viewed over time. When a new idea is presented, few individuals are likely to adopt it; then there is a spurt in the adoption rate as a significant number of people begin to adopt. He furthered argued that the take-off part of that s-curve of adoption starts to occur when opinion leaders begin to use the idea. As noted by Everett M. Rogers, Tarde observed that an innovation is first adopted by a person who is socially nearer to the source of the new idea and then it spreads. In propositional form, the more similar an innovation is to ideas that have already been accepted, the more likely the innovation is to be adopted (Rogers 1983).

The diffusion process was explored through the lenses of a number of different disciplines. Anthropologists analyzed how new ideas such as the steel ax, the boiling of water and the wheel had influenced and changed societies. Scholars of education examined innovations in learning, and those in marketing examined the impact of innovations like the touch-tone phone, clothing fashions and other new products. The theoretical ideas of Tarde were transformed into the measurement of innovation. Metrics were developed to allow scholars to understand the diffusion process better and begin to compare the impacts of the change process.

Most explicitly and directly following Tarde's theoretical ideas, scholars in the field of rural sociology began to study the entire process of how new technologies are introduced into communities and how those technologies change the economic nature of communities. These researchers took the lead in diffusion research because their discipline analyzed how new technologies and ideas moved from the laboratory to the market as a result of the American county agricultural agent model. Rural sociologists working in the laboratories of the agricultural schools of land-grant universities teach students, conduct scientific research to enhance farm production and interact within a significant ecosystem that includes the state agriculture agent. The agents are therefore responsible for the diffusion of innovations from the laboratory to the market. In this sense, agriculture was the first system that depended on university laboratories for research, the subsequent transformation of that research into business opportunities, and the development of a business ecosystem that entailed the dynamics of technology transfer and business creation. As perhaps the most successful technology transfer mechanism ever developed in the United States, the county agricultural agent model has successfully transferred an enormous amount of agricultural research to the American farmer and historically it has enabled America to feed the world. This particular ecosystem, especially during the heyday of the family farm, was composed primarily of suppliers, producers and competitors, with a variety of other stakeholders.

Thus diffusion theory, arising from different disciplines but especially rural sociology, became useful for research on technology clusters, rate of adoption of innovation, and the importance of opinion leaders and change agents. All these elements would reappear later as scholars created models to explain the emergence of more broadly based business ecosystems (Butler n.d.).

Business Clusters and Ecosystems

Diffusion theory at its core is concerned with how new ideas and technology innovations are integrated into society. As an extension of the diffusion approach, business ecosystem theory can be divided into two parts. The first part is concerned with how firms cluster and create ecosystems in order to compete better. The second is concerned with how certain parts of the country have become home to specific types of business clusters and how communities foster the development of new firms to join clusters. This literature falls under the rubric of regional competition or the technopolis. In business ecosystems, the unit of analysis is the firm. When looking at regional development, the unit of analysis is the region or the city. Although these two theories are distinct, in the literature there is overlap between them.

Cluster theory can be traced to Alfred Marshall, who noted that industries tend to cluster in distinct geographic districts, and that individual cities tend to specialize in the production of narrowly related kinds of goods (Marshall 1920). Marshall believed that knowledge spillovers are the cause of this clustering because they create a situation where trade secrets are not really secrets but rather information circulating in the air. Clustering also creates dense markets for specialized skills and the backward and forward linkages associated with large local markets.

Joseph Schumpeter continued down this theoretical pathway when he wrote that major innovations have historically tended to distribute themselves irregularly over time in clusters, bunches or swarms. Schumpeter's focus was on innovative breakthroughs in a major sector, those which gradually attract new firms into that sector to exploit the demonstrated profitability of the innovation (Schumpeter 1934). Although scholars from many disciplines have utilized cluster theory, we are concerned here with the theory's application to the business world as a theoretical tool for understanding strategy and community building.

Michael Porter's *The Competitive Advantage of Nations* introduced the idea of clusters as a way to explain successful competitive strategy (Porter 1990). James F. Moore's *The Death of Competition: Leadership and Strategy in the Age of Business Ecosystems* continued in this tradition (Moore 1996). Both Porter's and Moore's work has launched a literature that combines the early ideas of Everett Rogers on diffusion with insights about the competitive nature of the business world. This literature concludes that:

1. there is a relationship between geographic proximity and the driving of competition;
2. a market that is centered around an idea stimulates innovation;
3. entrepreneurial companies have access to suppliers, which allows them to compete with larger companies;
4. the bunching or clustering of companies draws investment funds;
5. this clustering encourages collaboration and diffusion of best practices between firms; and
6. clusters are a magnet for talented people.

According to Moore:

> To extend a systematic approach to strategy, I suggest that a company be viewed not as a member of a single industry but as part of a business ecosystem that crosses a variety of businesses. In a business ecosystem, companies co-evolve capabilities around a new innovation, they work cooperatively and competitively to support new products, satisfy customer needs, and eventually incorporate the next round of innovations. (Moore 1993, 76)

Companies such as IBM, Intel, Microsoft, SAP, Dell and Hewlett-Packard have incorporated this strategy of clusters as a competitive strategy. The role of the university as a driver of cluster or ecosystem creation is notably limited in earlier discussions of these approaches.

Regional Advantage Business Ecosystems and Clusters

George Kozmetsky's career spanned industry and academia. He was the co-founder and former executive vice-president of Teledyne and later the dean of the College of Business Administration and the Graduate School of Business at The University of Texas at Austin. He founded the IC^2 (Innovation, Creativity and Capital) Institute in 1977 as a platform for the demonstration of the use of science and technology as resources for economic development and enterprise growth. In 1993 Kozmetsky was a professor of management and serving as the director of IC^2. That year he presented a paper at the MIT Enterprise Forum that would enter the concept of the region, or community, into the cluster formula. While his ideas overlapped with the cluster analysis that took the firm as the unit of analysis, Kozmetsky's analysis brought out the importance of the interaction between the firm and community support. At the core of his analysis was not just the established firm but also the deliberate creation of new firms through a process that connects academia, government and business. As described in his paper 'Breaking the mold: reinventing business through community collaboration': 'The solutions to many critical issues and problems now demand an integrated, holistic flexible approach that blends technology, management, and scientific, socio-economic, cultural and political ramifications in an atmosphere of profound change and extreme time compression' (Kozmetsky 1993).

Kozmetsky's speech was given in the context of an economic culture where major American corporations, including the automobile, steel and other industries, were feeling the pressure of international competition. In response, new industries were being created using new organizational approaches that augmented the business cluster model with its approach of placing the firm at the center. These new organizational approaches included community or regional dynamics and the importance of new venture creation. At their hub was the research university where faculty members and students reinvigorated the American economy by enhancing job and wealth creation. While the old economies of the industrial Midwest were declining, a different kind of business model was emerging. Kozmetsky's type of model was already well under way in an area that had been agricultural but soon would be renamed Silicon Valley. In *Cloning Silicon Valley,* David Rosenberg wrote:

> Over the past two decades California's Silicon Valley has come to mesmerize the world. Like the great textile mills of Lancashire, America's trans-continental railways, or the Japanese automobile industry each in their day, California's cluster of high-technology companies and their supporting cast of universities, financiers and the like symbolize a bright new era. (Rosenberg 2002)

The vision for this model came not from an entrepreneur in the business world but rather from a Stanford professor, Frederick Terman, dean of engineering and provost at Stanford University. His vision was to make the university a major partner in economic development. Terman envisioned an aggressively entrepreneurial culture, which he called the newly emerging community of technical scholars, and which would combine academia and government for the transfer of knowledge from university laboratories to the business world.

From a historical and theoretical point of view, Terman's vision was a transfer of the agriculture diffusion model that had helped make America the agricultural capital of the world. As mentioned above, land-grant universities and their agricultural laboratories were at the apex of the knowledge and know-how that guided the development of new agricultural techniques and products. With few exceptions, universities did not usually play a direct role in economic development. But those exceptions are notable. Rensselaer Polytechnic Institute was created in the early 1800s, 'for the purpose of instructing persons . . . in the application of science to the common purposes of life' (Rensselaer Polytechnic Institute 2009). Another exception was the Tuskegee Institute, where the visionary Booker T. Washington combined science and technology to create industries for job and wealth creation from 1881 until his death in 1915. In accordance with the diffusion model, Tuskegee utilized the research of George Washington Carver to create and improve industries related to agriculture, thus making Tuskegee one of the first academic institutions to combine science and technology for wealth creation (McMurry 1981).

More recently researchers studying Silicon Valley, considered as an icon of a new way of doing business, have tried to define the variables that created and sustained that region. Every account highlights the importance of Stanford University. In *The Silicon Valley Edge: A Habitat for Innovation and Entrepreneurship,* James Gibbons, former dean of the Engineering School, deconstructs Stanford's contributions to the creation of Silicon Valley (Gibbons 2000). In addition to the traditional university function of supplying firms with graduates, he emphasizes the importance of entrepreneurial firms or start-ups. He assesses the requirements for successful start-ups (team-building, sources of capital, relationships between large industrial firms and start-ups, technical educational and social infrastructure) and the ways that the university attempted to meet these needs.

Research has also shown how Stanford interacted with other organizations to support start-up activities in the creation of Silicon Valley, including playing an important role in connecting entrepreneurs to venture capital, providing accountants who are knowledgeable about business start-up and growth, creating business deals, advising the new economy, interacting with inventors, building networks, attracting immigrant entrepreneurs and devising strategy. Annalee Saxenian's comparison of Silicon

Valley, viewed as a dynamic new form of business infrastructure, and Route 128 in Boston, which was declining in innovative productivity, helped shape research on the importance of the partnership between business communities and universities (Saxenian 1994).

The explosion of research and action designed to create the analog of Silicon Valley has been global and systematic. Under the general topic of technology clusters, several regions, including Cambridge, England; Hsinchu-Taipei, Taiwan; Singapore; Bangalore, India; Tel Aviv, Israel; and Helsinki, Finland, have been examined as to their attempts to replicate Silicon Valley. Additional areas examined include other nations in Asia, with a concentration on Vietnam, China and Japan (Kuchiki and Tsuji 2005). Following close on the heels of these studies were 'how-to' books for the development of the relationship between community dynamics and the economic success of communities (Porter 2001). The Austin model represents an important experiment in combining the lessons of diffusion theory with the theory of technology clusters.

Austin, Texas: theoretical application
The Austin model applies diffusion theory to the development of a business ecosystem designed to support entrepreneurial processes and outcomes, including job and wealth creation. Unlike other regions, the stakeholders designed and executed a plan for a model that was grounded in systematic research and intended to transform the entire region.

The Silicon Hills Technopolis: Early Experiments of the IC² Institute

The emergence of Austin as a high-tech center was so rapid and striking that Harvard Business School created a case study so that others might learn from the region's experience. The case study on Austin notes the importance of Silicon Valley's method of combining university expertise with science to produce an economy (Scott and Sunder 1998). If Silicon Valley was sliced out of the agricultural land of California, Austin was stretched out of the rock and rivers of the hill country of Texas. According to the case study: 'A concept pioneered at the IC² Institute was that of the "Technopolis Framework," a paradigm of technology-driven economic development. The framework emphasized interlocking relationships between academia, business and government . . . Austin was supposed to be a case in point of the technopolis framework in action' (ibid. 8). The case explicitly acknowledges Kozmetsky's contribution to theory and practice, even entitling one section, 'Kozmetsky's Technopolis'. Scholars associated with the IC² Institute created a theoretical road map for the technopolis that was designed to leverage science from The University of

Texas at Austin by using resources from national scientific laboratories, wealthy Texas families, government and industry.

The theoretical work done on diffusion and economic growth within the IC^2 Institute was impressive. One notable researcher was Everett Rogers, who took the discussion of diffusion theory from research on rural sociology to business application, and was an IC^2 research fellow. A later work, W.W. Rostow's *Theories of Economic Growth from David Hume to the Present*, contained a footnote about the theory that was developing in Austin (Rostow 1990). As an economist, Rostow was attempting to understand the relationship among new ideas and technology and growth, a relationship that was troublesome to some economists. He noted that: 'As of the 1980s, the IC^2 Institute at The University of Texas at Austin has evolved as a major center for the exploration of technological innovation and diffusion' (ibid. 647). He explored topics such as technological innovation and growth, industrial innovation, productivity and employment, commercializing technologies, technology venturing, transformation management, and innovation diffusion models and new product development.

Kozmetsky's 1993 MIT paper presentation allowed him to more broadly share the specifics of what was dubbed the Austin model, which he referred to as the experiment of IC^2 Fellows. This model was the embodiment of the IC^2 founding purpose, which was to:

> provide a structure for academia, business, and government to work in concert for the common good. To some extent today, business does not have confidence and trust in the government, nor does the government have confidence and trust in business. Both business and government believe that the academic sector cannot provide practical results in the short term. The major research task that the IC^2 Institute undertook in 1979 was to determine how our society could go about building confidence, cooperation, and collaboration among our institutions, especially for economic growth and job creation based on commercializing science and technology. (Kozmetsky 1993, 4–5)

For this reason the early research at the IC^2 Institute centered on institutional arrangements for new linkages among government, business and academia and included the identification and analysis of such emerging arrangements. Table 5.1 shows 16 collaborative competitive tools and their major purposes in the process from idea creation to diffusion of research for economic growth. As these institutional arrangements developed, many of them had different sponsors. The federal government served as a catalyst for university–industry–government research on topics such as supercomputing and manufacturing centers, intellectual property licensing, national technology initiatives, strategic partnerships and joint research and development (R&D) activities. State government fostered

Table 5.1 Sixteen collaborative competitive tools and their major purposes

Transfer models	Major purpose					
	For US scientific and economic sectors	To develop and maintain emerging industries	To create small and take-off companies	To improve US world-class manufacturing	Training	Leveraged economic development state/community
1. Consortia and alliances	✓	✓			✓	
2. Academic and business collaborations	✓					
3. University/industry/government research & engineering & manu.	✓			✓	✓	
4. Intellectual property licensing		✓	✓	✓		
5. University/business/government collaborations	✓	✓		✓		
6. Technology incubator	✓		✓		✓	✓
7. SBIRs			✓			
8. State venture funds		✓	✓			✓
9. Risk capital network		✓	✓			✓
10. Collaborative entrepreneurship			✓			
11. Federal lab government programs	✓	✓				

Table 5.1 (continued)

Transfer models	Major purpose					
	For US scientific and economic sectors	To develop and maintain emerging industries	To create small and take-off companies	To improve US world-class manufacturing	Training	Leveraged economic development state/community
12. Joint production venture						
13. Teaching/learning factories				✓	✓	
14. National technology initiatives	✓					✓
15. Enabling technologies and strategic partnerships		✓		✓		
16. Joint R&D (government/ individual joint missions)	✓	✓				

the development of state venture funds as well as supporting various kinds of academic and business collaborations. Industry created consortia and alliances with financial support from both federal and state government. Research at the IC² Institute revealed that newer institutional alliances were sometimes surrogates for national industrial policies and other government initiatives to encourage scientific research, enhance diffusion through technology transfer and generally create an ecosystem that fostered the success of private enterprise. Indeed the major purpose of the Austin regional alliances was to be a catalyst to unite academic and business institutions for diffusion of innovations that flowed from a process founded on cooperation and collaboration (Kozmetsky 1993, 5).

THE DEVELOPMENT OF THE AUSTIN MODEL

The IC² Institute launched the Austin model experiment, using these collaborative competitive tools, in 1989. With the Austin region as its laboratory, the IC² Institute devised a strategy to pull government, businesses and academic institutions together to build technology-based firms. Two primary goals drove the experiment. First, these firms were expected to create high-paying jobs within three years. A second and more short-term goal was to fill 1 million square feet of empty office space in Austin by 1999. Figure 5.1 illustrates the methodology of the Austin model. This illustration makes apparent the similarities to the early diffusion research. However in this case the starting point is the formulation of unstructured problems, those that have not been addressed before. The next steps are application research, concept development, experimental implementation and proactive dissemination, with the model eventually flowing back to the newly arisen, or at least newly identified, unstructured problems or anomalies that have appeared in the process of working through the model. The key concepts underlying the Austin model are these strategies for economic development: develop leadership and success factors that link government, business and academic sectors for cooperation and coordination; establish a robust community infrastructure of talent, technology, capital and know-how; and develop and report metrics for benchmarking and dissemination of progress.

The actual strategies underlying these concepts are presented in Figure 5.2. Writing earlier in his career, Kozmetsky had pointed out that industrial relocation had been the dominant strategy during the economic development of both the Sun Belt and the Rust Belt. This strategy can also be seen during the second Industrial Revolution, during which we saw companies resize as globalization and foreign competition became

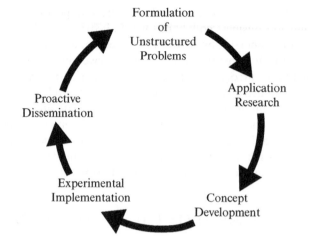

Source: IC² Institute Archives and PowerPoint Collection, The University of Texas at Austin.

Figure 5.1   The IC² approach for the Austin model

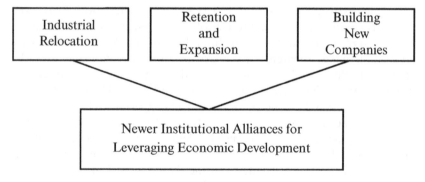

Figure 5.2   Strategies for economic development

more intense. The third Industrial Revolution was dominated by retention and expansion, and was anchored by technologies based on chemicals, combustion engines and electricity. These technologies produced goods that lasted from 20 to 40 years. Kozmetsky predicted that new companies would forge new institutional alliances to create the next revolution:

> Today's fourth Industrial Revolution technologies have a life cycle of no more than 12 to 36 months before technical obsolescence. They also experience intense competition at home and abroad. While building new companies is

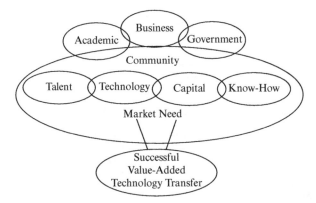

Source: IC² Institute Archives and PowerPoint Collection, The University of Texas at Austin.

Figure 5.3 Success factors for technology transfer

an important way for exploiting these newer technologies of microelectronics, telecommunications, biotechnology, lasers, and new materials, it still takes five to ten years before new companies become globally competitive. More rapid acceleration of new innovation requires leveraging economic developments that deal with new technology breakthroughs via consortia and alliances. (Kozmetsky 1993, 8)

Figure 5.3 shows the original diffusion model representing the movement of technologies from the lab to market with academic, business, government and community support. In such models, leadership must come from all sectors. The community infrastructure provides additional types of champions of wealth creation as well as strong entrepreneurs. This means that resource providers such as law firms, accounting firms, financial service firms and marketing firms are also significant in this equation. They help make up the public–private infrastructures that support the diffusion flow of new technologies to the marketplace.

Figure 5.4 moves the view of the Austin IC² diffusion model from the theoretical to the actionable, illustrating the emphasis on creating new companies. As part of the model three institutional alliances were created by the IC² Institute: (1) the Austin Technology Incubator (ATI); (2) the Texas Capital Network; and (3) the Texas Technology Incubator. The ATI was founded as a laboratory so that researchers could learn the process of systematic company creation and develop best practices. It was designed so that graduate students from all disciplines could interact with private companies in an organized setting. It also allowed The University

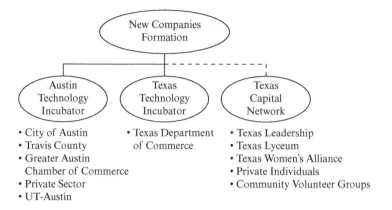

Source: IC² Institute Archives and PowerPoint Collection, The University of Texas at Austin.

*Figure 5.4   The Austin model: The University of Texas at Austin/IC²
experimental implementation*

of Texas at Austin and the IC² Institute to create a synergy between the Greater Austin Chamber of Commerce, the City of Austin, and the Texas Department of Commerce. More importantly the IC² Institute created a know-how network to codify and bring to the tenant companies the elements related to technology transfer, for example management, legal, finance and marketing talent.

Table 5.2 shows selected firms admitted to the ATI from June 1989 to December 1992, including the name of the company, the origin of the technology, the status during those years and the forecast. For example it can be seen that Pencom Software was admitted in June 1989, and that the technology originated with the entrepreneur. The product was custom software and the company had 85 employees. The capital investment was $2 million, and the forecast was for graduated annual sales of over $40 million. Since the time of these early experiments, the ATI has continued to be a laboratory for graduate students from every discipline and to carry out its original mission. Since its inception it has launched over 150 companies, raised over $750 million dollars in investor capital for member companies, created four companies with initial public offerings and made many significant acquisitions. Three member or recent-graduate companies are listed in Deloitte & Touche's Texas Fast 50 list of the fastest-growing Texan companies.

The Texas Capital Network (TCN), which was housed in the ATI, was created so that Texans could learn the process of investing in high-

Table 5.2   List of selected firms, Austin Technology Incubator, June 1989–December 1992

Company	Origin			Product	Current status		Forecast/ activity
	Entry date	Source of technology	Number of employees		Number of employees	Capital invested	
Information technology database software							
Evolutionary Technologies, Inc.	Jan. 91	MCC	5	Extract database conversion toolkit	30	$2 M from venture capital	Building distribution channels
Third Coast Software	Mar. 90	Own idea	1	Object-oriented process control sw	4	Prepaid licenses – AMD, Motorola	Early in sales cycle
System software							
Rainbow Analysis Group	Oct. 91	Own idea	1	Tools for building fault-tolerant hw	5	Self-financed	–
Pencom Software	Jun. 89	Own idea	1	Custom software	85	$2 M – internal	Graduated Annual sales over $40M

Table 5.2 (continued)

Company	Origin			Current status			Forecast/ activity
	Entry date	Source of technology	Number of employees	Product	Number of employees	Capital invested	
Haystack Laboratories	Jun. 91	Funded research government agencies	1	Security	3	Contractual financing and Angel	–
Decision support software			1				
Collaborative Technologies, Inc.	Oct. 90	University	5	VisionQuest groupware	12	$2.5 M from venture capital	Expanding sales activity – raising second-round financing
Corporate Memory Systems, Inc.	Nov. 91	MCC	6	CM/I groupware	11	$0.6 M – Angel	Won Best of Show award – Groupware 91
Logical Information Machines	Jan. 90	Own idea	1	LIM (Knowledge mining database)	9	$0.7 M – Angel	Market-security industry
Expert Application Systems, Inc.	May. 90	Own idea	1	Expert system sw	7	–	–

Semiconductor manufacturing							
Fourth State Technologies	Apr. 92	SEMATECH	2	Sensor-based feedback for manufacturing	1	–	Looking for manufacturer
Linden Technology	Mar. 92	University	1	Design for Gig DRAW	1	Seed capital only	–
Computer hardware							
DTM	Aug. 89	University	2	3-D prototype machine	102	$16 M by Fortune 100 company	Graduated potential strategic business unit for BF Goodrich
CompuSics	Nov. 91	Own idea	3	Seismic data processor	6	Self-financed	$2-4 M sales to Schlumberger acquisition candidate
Fusion Data	Oct. 90	Own idea and licensed MCC Technology	3	Mac upgrade board	8	$100 K	Selling in Europe and Pacific Rim
HaL Computers	Feb. 91	Own idea and Fujitsu	1	Proprietary UNIX hardware	52	$40 M	Largest US start-up

Table 5.2 (continued)

Company	Origin				Current status			Forecast/ activity
	Entry date	Source of technology	Number of employees	Product	Number of employees	Capital invested		
Telecommunications								
Rochelle	Oct. 89	Own idea	1	Caller ID	10	$300 K		Graduates first caller ID product
Optodigital Design	Nov. 89	Own idea	1	Medical lasers	5	$60 K		Awaiting FDA approval
Biomedical/medical								
Autogenesis	May. 91	Siberia, Community of Ind. States	1	Limb generation	2	$1.6 M		Pioneering product at critical sales cycle
Optomed	Nov. 89	Own idea	1	Medical lasers	5	$60 K		Awaiting FDA approval
CEDRA	Jun. 90	Own idea	2	Pharmaceutical testing	17	Contract financing		Annual sales $2 M
Encore Orthopedics	Apr. 92	Own idea	1	Orthopedic implants	37	$3 M from overseas		Developing manufacturing
Medical Polymer	May. 92	Technology acquisition from California	3	Disinfectant	9	$2 M IPO		FDA approval received August 1992

technology companies. In his role as advocate for the emerging ecosystem, Kozmetsky facilitated the launch of this network by driving throughout the state and holding meetings about investing. At that time TCN was the fastest-growing venture network in America. It was described in the following way in an IC² document:

> The TCN database lists more than one hundred investors who are interested in investing over 80 million dollars in promising ATI and other companies. These investors include individuals, venture-capital firms, economic-development funds, and corporate investors seeking joint venture or acquisition opportunities . . . Ventures are seeking from fifty thousand dollars to more than fifteen million dollars in funding . . . Start-ups comprise 30% of the ventures listed; another 50% are classified as 'emerging companies' from one to five years old. The remaining 20% are more than five years old. (Kozmetsky 1993, 20)

The Texas Technology Incubator, a precursor of the Texas Department of Commerce, was created in 1978 and was composed largely of civic entrepreneurs. The organization was designed to enhance the ability of the Texas region to be competitive. The creative strategy was to combine state agencies, which already existed, into an organization that would further enhance the ability of Texas to compete. Ultimately the model went even further when the Texas Economic Development Commission, the Texas World Trade Council, the Texas Enterprise Zone Board, the Technology Training Board, the Texas Film Commission and Texas Music Commission, and the Job Training Partnership Act were all combined to create the Texas Department of Commerce. The official purpose of the department was to plan, organize and implement programs to attract new businesses to the state, encourage the growth and expansion of existing businesses, including tourism, and work with local governments and organizations to improve their communities. In order to implement research, the department was responsible for maintaining all data related to economic development, including memos, résumés, economic development grants and special reports. In a real sense, they augmented the research efforts that were taking place at the IC² Institute and the Bureau of Business Research at The University of Texas Business School.

Research shows that other companies also developed as spin-outs of IC² companies. One example listed in the IC² archives is PC Limited, Inc., a company that predated the development of the ATI but still benefited from the know-how network of the IC² Institute and Kozmetsky. This company would evolve into Dell Computers. In his book *Direct from Dell: Strategies That Revolutionized an Industry*, Michael Dell wrote about Kozmetsky:

In trying to create a wish list of directors, we came up with two names: George Kozmetsky and Bob Inman. Both lived in Austin, had knowledge of the computer industry, and had very distinguished backgrounds. George was a cofounder of Teledyne and had served as dean of The University of Texas School of Business; Bob had been chairman, president, and CEO of Westmark Systems, a private defense company, and had extensive background in the federal government. . . . Their presence gave us a huge boost in credibility; young companies like Dell typically don't have such a strong board starting out. As the original Board members, George and Bob set a precedent of sage advice and valuable counsel that has helped carry us to where we are today. (Dell 1999, 21)

LESSONS LEARNED

The Austin model, developed by scholars at the IC^2 Institute at The University of Texas at Austin, was a case of applying theories of innovation and diffusion to the creation of companies and the transformation of the region. This model specified roles for business, government and educational institutions and successfully transformed Austin, Texas, and the surrounding region. Before the introduction of this diffusion model, using the early 1980s as a starting point, Austin's opportunities were provided by state government and the university. It was embedded in a cowboy ranching culture not known for high-tech jobs. With this kind of economic base, the city and region could not retain educational talent. Ten years later, the November 1996 issue of *Fortune* named Austin the best city in America for business and one of the top five cities for wealth creation. In 2000 *Forbes* named Austin one of the top 15 cities for entrepreneurship.

The story of how Austin interacted with the IC^2 Institute is just now entering the literature. According to Pike Powers, in a paper entitled 'Building the Austin technology cluster: the role of government and community collaboration in the human capital':

[Austin] is one of a handful of American cities that has become a true center for technology innovation. For the past three decades, the city's leadership – in business, government, and academia – has collaborated on a vision of Austin's future that solidly embraces science and technology. Austin is not a secret any longer. With more than 30 years experience attracting (and keeping) technology companies, Austin is home to more than 2200 technology companies, employing approximately 120000 of the region's workforce. With technology as the future . . . it is essential to stay competitive and collaborate. Redefining the role of all levels has made a huge difference for Austin. It can do so for other communities too. (Powers 2004, 1)

Powers's analysis shows how the Austin collaboration was instrumental in attracting institutions such as the Microelectronics and Computer

Technology Corporation (MCC), SEMATECH (a consortium that concentrates on semiconductor manufacturing), and in encouraging general targeted marketing to and recruitment of companies. Companies like Samsung, 3M, AMD, National Instruments and Motorola joined home-grown companies like Dell, Whole Foods, Tracor, Golfsmith and National Instruments.

As we continue to understand the influence and impact of the IC² Institute at The University of Texas at Austin, one could codify the lessons learned as follows:

1. The importance of a visionary. In order for a region or a community to reinvent itself, a visionary will play a major role. In the case of the Texas region, it is clear that George Kozmetsky was one of the people with vision who understood the importance of creating a technopolis.
2. The business world is not self-organizing. Our research makes it clear that helping to organize new and developing fields is very important for economic development. The IC² Institute helped organize the Austin Software Council, the Texas Capital Network and other organizations that create a synergy around economic development. These organizations also help with the diffusion of innovation process.
3. Technology transfer from laboratory to market is important for new venture creation, wealth creation and job creation. Any region or city can transform itself by concentrating on the relationship between science and economic development. It is certain that in the twenty-first century we will continue to see companies created and enhanced by taking scientific findings from the laboratory to the market. Biotechnology and nanotechnology should have a significant impact on wealth creation in the future.
4. Universities play a significant role in economic development. Federal funding for innovation has been partially moved to what are called major research universities. We must continue to combine business practices with science and engineering for economic development in the twenty-first century. Institutions like the IC² Institute must also continue to advance economic development around the globe by creating programs that diffuse the knowledge of wealth creation through technology transfer.
5. Make the entrepreneurs and wealthy people who are willing to invest heroes. One of the great lessons of Austin, Texas, is the importance of wealthy individuals and families who 'took a chance on the kids'. These individuals, although they might not have fully understood the technology revolution, listened to the new ideas and invested in them. Austin also created a culture where entrepreneurs were heroes. As described in a column in the *Austin American-Statesman* called

'Tech Monday', heroes were not only from the world of sports, but also people who created jobs and wealth. In an almost unprecedented way, Michael Dell (Dell Computers), John Mackey (Whole Foods), Carl Paul (Golfsmith), James Truchard (National Instruments) and Gary Hoover (Bookstop, Hoovers Online) became heroes as much as legendary Texan sports figures like Earl Campbell (Heisman Trophy winner, 1977), Darrell Royal (Longhorn coach, College Football Hall of Fame, 1983), Roger Clemens (World Series 1999, 2000) and Ben Crenshaw (The Masters, 1984, 1995).

CONCLUSION AND FUTURE MODELS OF ECONOMIC DEVELOPMENT

As Austin moves into the twenty-first century, it is living in the house that George Kozmetsky and the IC^2 Institute helped build. The Austin model for diffusion of science to create wealth and jobs has been tested and tried around the globe. Countries where scholars are measuring the effects of the model include China, the United Kingdom, India, Israel, Japan, Korea, Poland, Russia, Portugal, Iraq and the United States. Texas, because of the emergence of the Austin technopolis, is the only state that has committed over $200 million to enhancing technology transfer and wealth creation. As noted by Governor Rick Perry:

> In Texas, we understand that high-tech companies don't just happen overnight but are a product of forethought, sound vision and planning, and strategic investments by both the public and private sectors. Through our Emerging Technology Fund, we are bringing the best scientists and researchers to Texas, attracting high-tech jobs and helping start-up companies get off the ground faster. (Perry 2009)

The Fund works with universities throughout the state to ensure that companies receiving investment funds have been vetted so that business acceleration can take place. In a real sense, the Emerging Technology Fund of the State of Texas continues an experiment that was developed at the IC^2 Institute at The University of Texas at Austin.

REFERENCES

Butler, John Sibley (n.d.), 'County agent model for entrepreneurship', Working Paper, IC^2 Institute, The University of Texas at Austin, http://www.IC2.Utexas.edu/publications/county_agent_model.pdf.

Butler, John Sibley and David Gibson (forthcoming), *Global Perspectives on Technology Transfer and Commercialization: The IC² Impact*.

Dell, Michael (1999), *Direct From Dell: Strategies that Revolutionized an Industry*, New York: HarperBusiness.

Gibbons, James F. (2000), 'The role of Stanford University', in Chong Moon Lee, William Miller, Marguerite Hancock and Henry Rowen (eds), *The Silicon Valley Edge: A Habitat for Innovation and Entrepreneurship*, Palo Alto: Stanford University Press, pp. 200–217.

Kozmetsky, George (1993), 'Breaking the mold: reinventing business through community collaboration', Paper presented to the MIT Enterprise Forum, Cambridge, MA 23 October.

Kuchiki, Akifumi and Masatsugu Tsuji (eds) (2005), *Industrial Clusters in Asia: Analyses of their Competition and Corporation*, New York: Palgrave MacMillan.

Marshall, Alfred (1920), *Principles of Economics*, London: Macmillan.

McMurry, Linda O. (1981), *George Washington Carver: Scientist and Symbol*, Oxford: Oxford University Press.

Moore, James F. (1993), 'Predators and prey: a new ecology of competition', *Harvard Business Review*, May–June: 75–86.

Moore, James F. (1996), *The Death of Competition: Leadership and Strategy in the Age of Business Ecosystems*, New York: HarperBusiness.

Perry, Rick (2009), Texas Emerging Technology 'About the Emerging Technology Fund', Website, Fund http://members.texasone.us/site/PageServer?pagename=tetf_homepage (accessed 8 June 2009).

Porter, Michael E. (1990), *The Competitive Advantage of Nations*, New York: Free Press.

Porter, W. Arthur (2001), *The Knowledge Seekers: How to Turn your Community into an Engine for Economic Success*, Austin, TX: IC² Fellows Book Series.

Powers, Pike (2004), 'Building the Austin technology cluster: the role of government and community collaboration in the human capital', *Proceedings, Rural Conferences*, Federal Reserve Bank of Kansas City.

Rensselaer Polytechnic Institute (2009), 'About Rensselaer Polytechnic Institute (RPI)', http://www.rpi.edu/about/index.html (accessed 1 June 2009).

Rogers, Everett M. (1983), *Diffusion of Innovations*, 3rd edn, New York: Free Press.

Rosenberg, David (2002), *Cloning Silicon Valley: The Next Generation High-Tech Hotspots*, London: Pearson Education.

Rostow, W.W. (1990), *Theories of Economic Growth from David Hume to the Present*, New York: Oxford University Press.

Saxenian, Annalee (1994), *Regional Advantage: Culture and Competition in Silicon Valley and Route 128*, Cambridge, MA: Harvard University Press.

Schumpeter, Joseph (1934), *Theory of Economic Development*, Cambridge, MA: Harvard University Press.

Scott, Bruce R. and Srinivas Sunder (1998), 'Austin, Texas: building a high-tech economy', Harvard Business School, case number 9-799-038 Cambridge, MA: President and Fellows of Harvard College.

Smilor, Raymond W., George Kozmetsky and David V. Gibson (1998), *Creating the Technopolis: Linking Technology Commercialization and Economic Development*, Cambridge, MA: Harper & Row.

Tarde, Gabriel de (1903), *The Laws of Imitation*, trans. Elsie Clews Parsons, New York: H. Holt & Company.

6. Tecnológico de Monterrey

Jose Manuel Aguirre Guillén, Arturo Torres García and Karla Giordano

DESCRIPTION OF THE ENTREPRENEURSHIP ECOSYSTEM

The likelihood that entrepreneurs will successfully grow their businesses depends not only on their motivation but also on their capabilities and the opportunities available in their environment. Entrepreneurship is a difficult activity to cultivate because it demands so many different supporting components to move from an idea or concept to successful execution. The sum of such components, when properly organized and harmoniously interacting with each other, becomes the ecosystem.

If promoting entrepreneurship in developed countries is hard, in developing countries the task is even more difficult due to a number of barriers such as unwelcoming attitudes in society, the lack of training and mentors, the lack of access to credit and financing, and the lack of access to innovation and research resources (Curtin 2003).

The Mexican Context

Over the past years Mexico's competitive position in several global rankings has been moving downward. Although in general terms gross domestic product (GDP) and inflation have shown stability and steady growth, the speed and the response to accelerated growth in nations like Korea, China or India have been insufficient. As in other Latin American countries, the Mexican economy has been supported by low- to middle-level value-added processes like manufacturing and natural resources. In addition, insufficient investment in research and development (R&D) has led to a significant weakness in product and process innovation. R&D expenditure, although rising from 0.3 percent in 2001 to 0.5 percent of GDP in 2007, is still low by international standards (Mittelstädt and Cerri 2009).

According to a European Commission report on Mexico's future:

Mexico's future development will increasingly have to be based on the effective generation and utilization of knowledge, in order to meet economic, social and environmental challenges. The role of the scientific and technological communities in knowledge supply and in its effective integration in innovation systems cannot be overemphasized. If it wants to invest coherently in its own S&T assets, and assert its own intellectual and scientific capacities in the global knowledge society, Mexico must strive to go beyond the level of being an 'economic province' of the much larger and US-dominated NAFTA [North American Free Trade Agreement]. (European Commission 2002)

Mexico is currently facing a radical shift in its economic backbone. Federal and state governments are looking for alternatives to economic development, with a particular emphasis on high-value activities, sustainability and long-term competitiveness. Knowledge-based development has been identified as a core constituent of any model. Over the past few years Mexico has increasingly emphasized entrepreneurship policy as a principal means of stimulating innovation (Mittelstädt and Cerri 2009). Entrepreneurship abounds in Mexico but is concentrated among low-risk, low-value-added endeavors that require minimum investments of capital; furthermore the 2006 Global Entrepreneurship Monitor (GEM) report found that 5 percent of Mexicans are involved in entrepreneurial activities, a fall from the 18 percent reported in 2002. Nevertheless, small and medium-sized enterprises (SMEs) play a vital role in Mexico's economy. They are estimated to account for about 99 percent of all enterprises generating 52 percent of the GDP in 2006 and represent nearly three-quarters of total employment (GEM 2006).

Although universities have been part of Mexican society, their role in regional development has not yet reached its full potential. Tecnológico de Monterrey has been leading several efforts to drive and revolutionize the Mexican entrepreneurial ecosystem.

The business incubation scenario in Mexico

Business incubation activities emerged in Mexico during the 1990s, a decade after the attention earned by business incubators in the 1980s, particularly in the United States. The first experience with business incubation was promoted by federal agencies like the National Council for Science and Technology (CONACyT) and the Secretary of the Economy. They were seen as mechanisms to foster employment and business generation. Unfortunately these early initiatives did not succeed, and most of the first incubators ceased to exist. Science and technology parks endured a similar fate. The Science Parks initiative of CONACyT in the 1990s could not achieve the desired results, mostly due to the lack of appropriate operational models and sustainable financial strategies (Corona et al. 2006).

Business incubation activities had their second and perhaps more successful introduction beginning in 2000. This time universities (Tecnológico de Monterrey among others) proposed a new configuration, operational models and management for the business incubators. According to the National System for Business Incubation, in 2009 there were 324 incubators in Mexico, with 18 devoted to high-technology firms. Tecnológico de Monterrey pioneered this new wave of incubation developments with a new indigenous model. This model has succeeded partially because of the entrepreneurial programs established at the institution 20 years earlier and also because of the unique national position of the university. Tecnológico de Monterrey has 106 incubators in Mexico and has transferred its model (which is officially certified by the Mexican government) to a significant number of national and Latin American universities.

Science and technology parks, as well as the explicitly technology-based business incubators, have also had a rebirth, this time propelled by their impressive growth in many regions of the world and their noticeable role in the newest knowledge-based economic development models. Universities, again, have been promoting these efforts. Although some states have initiated the planning of technology parks, for example, Nuevo Leon, Jalisco and Baja California, Tecnológico de Monterrey's strategy has earned top status, including backing from the Ministry of the Economy, which is committed to supporting more than 20 projects currently being planned. Nuevo Leon, the state where Tecnológico de Monterrey was founded and where its larger campus is located, has been a key region to test strategies and disseminate the successful experiences.

Tecnológico de Monterrey

Tecnológico de Monterrey is a private university system comprising 33 campuses in several Mexican cities, a virtual university that covers Mexico and Latin America, plus 12 liaison offices in America, Europe and Asia (Bustani et al. 2006). Tecnológico de Monterrey was founded in 1943 by local industrial leaders as a non-profit organization independent of politics or religion. More than 60 years later, Tecnológico de Monterrey is one of the most highly recognized institutions of higher learning in Latin America and around the world. It enrolls around 88 000 high school, undergraduate and graduate students, including 400 PhD students. The faculty numbers approximately 8000, of which around 3000 are full-time and 1200 have PhDs. Tecnológico de Monterrey enjoys international student exchange agreements with more than 300 universities and cooperates in research with more than 50 universities worldwide.

As a leading university, Tecnológico de Monterrey is committed to playing a key role in the regional development strategies of Mexico. Because the global economic landscape is driven primarily by knowledge and high-value-based enterprises, Tecnológico de Monterrey has established several regional development programs that nurture business activities built on promising technologies and advanced industrial sectors like information technology (IT) and biotechnology. Some of these programs have been attracted by and contribute to other technology-based companies in the region.

As a result of the institutional vision defined for 2015, Tecnológico de Monterrey has made a commitment to contribute to Mexico's development through four core strategies:

- competitiveness based on the knowledge economy;
- job creation;
- strengthening public administration and public policy;
- reduction of the educational gap.

To fulfill this vision, Tecnológico de Monterrey has developed high-value programs and infrastructure that spur technology-based enterprise development. In order to achieve these goals, Tecnológico de Monterrey is looking for global leaders in key areas of knowledge and technology to cultivate a wealthier and more dynamic economy for companies, communities and regions.

Tecnológico de Monterrey innovation ecosystem strategy
The vision of Tecnológico de Monterrey has permeated its R&D activities by aspiring to the following goals:

- foster sustainable regional development;
- capitalize knowledge for society's benefit;
- develop innovation-provoking environments;
- provide faculty and students with the experience of technology transfer, technology commercialization and business incubation;
- consolidate Tecnológico de Monterrey as an academic, scientific and entrepreneurial ally.

In order to reach these five goals, Tecnológico de Monterrey has expanded and consolidated its activities in the following ten strategic programs, some of which are of recent creation. The emphasis on these programs will position it as a leader in innovation, technological development and sustainable development in Mexico and Latin America:

1. greater development of human capital;
2. expansion of graduate programs;
3. increased number of research chairs;
4. creation of research centers of excellence;
5. integration of research networks;
6. integration of technological development networks;
7. integration of industrial support networks;
8. establishment of business incubators and accelerators;
9. creation and promotion of technology parks;
10. conversion of campuses into sustainable campuses.

Research and development, business incubators and accelerators, and technology parks are three core elements of the ecosystem.

The Impulse toward R&D Activities

The innovation ecosystem strategy of Tecnológico de Monterrey is a commitment to the competitive development of all regions of Mexico, based on research, development, innovation and the incubation of ideas. The formulation of such a strategy considers a regional, national and international context, which requires a focus on the priorities of each region while also taking into account the greater social and technological tendencies in the world (Molina et al. 2008). Tecnológico de Monterrey has defined five goals for R&D strategy:

1. Increase scientific and technological research that addresses the social, economic, cultural and knowledge-transfer demands at the national level.
2. Train researchers and PhDs in diverse disciplines according to national and regional needs.
3. Increase the interaction of Tecnológico de Monterrey with national and international scientific systems and their connection to the productive sector.
4. Increase R&D activities as well as the capacity for innovation and incubation of the productive sector through the transfer of technology.
5. Support and favor collaboration and cooperation between the key agents for the I+D+i2 Strategy as a way to encourage the creation and development of regional systems of innovation that facilitate the creation and distribution of wealth.

The Business Incubation Model

The business incubation model (Torres et al. 2007) of Tecnológico de Monterrey described in this section has been recognized by the federal Ministry of the Economy.

The three stages of the incubation model

The business incubation model of Tecnológico de Monterrey has three stages that entrepreneurs must complete: creation, development and consolidation of corresponding businesses. The model provides support for entrepreneurs at each stage.

The first stage, pre-incubation, consists of helping a person who has an entrepreneurial spirit express an idea in a business plan. This plan should include the company's feasibility, a marketing plan, finances, administration, operation and legal matters. This stage ends with a well-founded business plan and the legal incorporation of the company.

In the second stage of this model, incubation, the company starts operation on a small scale, finds customers and suppliers, issues invoices and copes with all the typical challenges faced by any company that is operational. Post-incubation, the third stage of the model, occurs when the company has achieved a satisfactory level of growth. The support offered by Tecnológico de Monterrey during this phase therefore concentrates primarily on the growth strategies and consolidation of the business.

This model and the services offered at each of its stages seek to fulfill three core objectives:

- To offer students, graduates and the entrepreneurial community a model for developing new businesses.
- To prepare nationally and internationally competitive business people and companies to contribute to the social development of the community.
- To enable the campuses of Tecnológico de Monterrey to contribute to the development of their sphere of influence.

Tutors and specialized advisors

The business incubator has a group of tutors and specialized advisors who accompany the entrepreneurs during their companies' creation and growth. The advisors who agree to participate in this group are generally highly experienced in the establishment of their own businesses or they work as consultants for medium-sized and small companies.

Each person who is incubating a company is assigned a tutor. The tutors are not necessarily experts in the same line of business for which they advise. Nevertheless they have the necessary skills to monitor the companies, motivate the new entrepreneurs and help them manage and execute each of the stages of the incubation model. The tutors represent a moral authority for the people who are starting up a business.

The function of the specialized advisors is to strengthen specific areas of the new business. Specialized advisors from the following six areas are assigned to each incubating company: administration and organization, marketing and sales, foreign trade, accounting and finances, production and manufacturing, and legal matters. In some cases, entrepreneurs are offered advice from experts who are highly specialized in the line of business in question, for example aeronautics, wind power and nutraceuticals. There are about 350 experts working as specialized tutors or advisors at the business incubator network of Tecnológico de Monterrey.

Face-to-face and virtual formats
The business incubators on Tecnológico de Monterrey campuses feature physical installations that include offices for the entrepreneurs, meeting rooms, service centers and common areas that foment a business atmosphere among the entrepreneurs and allow them to interact face-to-face with their tutors and specialized advisors. However all the participants in the process – advisees, tutors and advisors – are made to see the importance of interacting through the Emprendetec portal, the technological platform of the business incubator network, which is described in detail later in this chapter. Its purpose is to monitor, in real time and institution-wide, the progress made by each company and thus improve the incubation model day by day. The interaction that takes place on this platform makes it possible to detect areas of opportunity in the process and to monitor the response times of the tutors and specialized advisors, as well as the evaluations made by the entrepreneurs of the advice they receive, thus facilitating any necessary preventive actions.

Some of the smaller Tecnológico de Monterrey campuses do not have special facilities for entrepreneurs. In these cases, anyone who wants to incubate a business has the option of doing so through the Emprendetec portal, where they will receive remotely the support of their respective tutors and specialized advisors throughout the development of their companies. In the same way, the Emprendetec portal is available to entrepreneurs who do not live near a Tecnológico de Monterrey campus but wish to incubate their company.

The physical installations of the business incubators and the Emprendetec portal are undoubtedly highly valuable resources. Nevertheless, the decisive factor in the success of this program is its creation of an ecosystem that promotes the transfer of knowledge. With regard to the format offered to counsel entrepreneurs, the business incubators offer two types of membership: face-to-face and virtual. Both types of members have access to the Emprendetec portal, a tutor, specialized advisors, online training and links to businesses, through which they can make their products or services known among the business incubator network users. Face-to-face members can also make use of physical spaces, such as offices or cubicles, meeting rooms, training rooms and service centers, and access shared equipment.

Evaluation of the tutoring and specialized advisory services

In order to begin operating the business incubators, Tecnológico de Monterrey had to find tutors and specialized advisors. To this end the campuses identified entrepreneurs or consultants in their community who were close enough to Tecnológico de Monterrey to invite them to participate in this program. Tutors and specialized advisors go through an introductory program that includes learning the criteria by which their performance will be evaluated since those who are creating a company or receiving advice, either face-to-face or virtually, periodically evaluate the quality of the service provided by their assigned experts.

In the case of advice offered in the virtual format, the central administration of the business incubator network is responsible for following up on the results of these evaluations and tracking the average number of hours that the tutors or specialized advisors take to respond to entrepreneurs' questions, which should be no longer than 48 hours. The results of the evaluations of both the quality of the interaction with the tutors or specialized advisors and the response time make it possible to take action to ensure that experts in the business incubator network are offering effective support to the entrepreneurs.

The Emprendetec portal

As a result of the experience of Tecnológico de Monterrey in distance-education models for the preparation, training and education of its students, graduates and community members, the virtual incubation format was defined in 2002 as a strategic part of the model of the business incubator network. This format relied on the Emprendetec portal, a technological tool that would also support the face-to-face incubation format. The Emprendetec portal was released in May 2003, thereby making it possible for all Tecnológico de Monterrey incubators to offer the virtual format to their users.

The Emprendetec portal allows tutors and specialized advisors to interact with and provide services to future entrepreneurs, regardless of their location. It also offers the possibility of generating companies that are incubated entirely through virtual tutoring and advice, as described previously in this section.

Preparation of future business people

The Business Incubator Network offers six online courses that each last approximately nine hours and reinforce the entrepreneurs' basic knowledge of the relevant area of business. If the tutors or specialized advisors detect that one of the entrepreneurs needs to reinforce their basic knowledge of a specific area of business, they recommend that the entrepreneurs take courses that will enable them to strengthen their skills and benefit more from their subsequent interactions with the specialized advisors.

Business councils

The business incubation model requires the participation of different agents who contribute to the entrepreneurs' business education. Therefore Tecnológico de Monterrey has insisted on linking the business incubator network with the business sector, government organizations and organizations that support SMEs. This has resulted in the creation of business councils at each of the Tecnológico de Monterrey campuses.

The members, together with a network of tutors and specialized advisors, contribute their experience via suggestions, recommendations, contacts and other types of support to strengthen the growth process of the companies that are incubated at Tecnológico de Monterrey. These councils comprise leading business people from the local communities as well as representatives from state governments and other public organizations.

Duration of the incubation process

Pre-incubation covers a period of time that varies according to the type of company and how advanced the definition of the business idea is. This stage might last longer if the firm requires high technology in its processes. The second stage of incubation, during which entrepreneurs receive support to start operating their businesses, lasts between a year and a year and a half. After this period the post-incubation stage begins, during which the entrepreneurs can continue to receive services focused on consolidating their businesses for an indefinite length of time.

Incubator network for technology-based firms

Tecnológico de Monterrey seeks to contribute to sustainable development in diverse regions of Mexico through the efforts of a group of specialists and researchers from several fields who have been conducting research, consultancy and educational activities to boost the transformation of technological developments with a high level of market potential into sustainable businesses.

During the incubation process of this type of firm, the association between the business sector and the educational sector is fundamental. This creates the ideal conditions for Tecnológico de Monterrey to contribute to stimulating the development of a knowledge-based economy. The commitment of the institution to supporting the development of the country in this way is demonstrated in its vision statement for the year 2015, which states that Tecnológico de Monterrey will be the leading educational institution in Latin America, among other reasons, 'for its research and development work to further the knowledge-based economy'.

Incubator network for intermediate-technology firms
The business model for intermediate-technology firms includes elements of innovation in the processes, products or services they offer. The incubation model described in the section entitled 'The Business Incubation Model' was specifically designed for this type of company and is applied with great precision.

Incubator network for social companies (bottom of the pyramid)
Tecnológico de Monterrey initiated an effort in 2000 to support underprivileged and geographically isolated communities through community learning centers, learning spaces that primarily seek to offer a quality education to the inhabitants of these communities. Based on the experience acquired by Tecnológico de Monterrey at the community learning centers and in the business incubation processes, the Institute for Sustainable Social Development (IDeSS) emerged, with the principal objective of creating a social incubator network. The social incubators of Tecnológico de Monterrey use the traditional micro-company incubation model, which is an adaptation of the incubation model described in the section entitled 'The Business Incubation Model'. The adaptation of the business incubation model of Tecnológico de Monterrey for micro companies is possible because undergraduate students from Tecnológico de Monterrey provide consulting services for the social entrepreneurs. The students sometimes also act as specialized advisors but when the future entrepreneurs' problems go beyond their knowledge, the students can turn to experts from the other subnetworks for help. Through this student activity, the social incubators have become an essential instrument for Tecnológico de Monterrey to fulfill its mission of preparing citizens who 'are committed to the economic, political, social and cultural development of their communities'.

Students who are interested in becoming social tutors have to complete a course called Social Entrepreneurs instead of the traditional course,

Entrepreneurial Development. A fundamental component of this course is the tutoring performed by the students for people who are incubating a traditional micro company. The hours spent on this activity earn credit toward the students' social service requirement. Therefore the social incubators of the IDeSS represent laboratories in which Tecnológico de Monterrey students develop an attitude of community support while also putting into practice the knowledge acquired in their curriculum courses.

Through the course Social Entrepreneurs students are trained to:

- participate as social incubator promoters;
- be business plan development coaches;
- act as productive project tutors;
- identify market opportunities and recommend them to those who want to start up a new company.

Just like the other two types of incubator networks, social incubators offer face-to-face and virtual formats to support future business people.

Social incubators form part of Tecnológico de Monterrey's strategy to further the development of Mexico, since they foster the social advancement of the people who use them to create or enhance their companies. The expected end result is an elevation in their quality of life index, which leads to greater social inclusion.

Association with Institutions that Support SMEs

Government institutions

The rapid growth of the incubator network at Tecnológico de Monterrey has been made possible largely through support from the Ministry of the Economy, which created the Office for Micro-, Small- and Medium-sized Enterprise on the initiative of the federal government in 2000. This office developed the SME Fund, which seeks to support through diverse financial incentives the institutions that serve these types of companies. The main incentives include financial support for:

- infrastructure and equipment of new business incubators;
- business training and instruction;
- consulting provided by experts from diverse lines of business;
- technological innovation and development;
- market surveys;
- organization of business-oriented events;
- generation of clusters;
- granting seed money for entrepreneurs;

- development of technology parks;
- creation of business angels clubs.

Resources granted by the federal government normally have to be matched by the economic development offices of the diverse states of Mexico. The agreement also requires that Tecnológico de Monterrey contribute its own important economic resources. The institute also works hand-in-hand with public organizations at all levels of the government from which it might obtain benefits for the generation of companies. These organizations include municipal offices, the Mexican Institute for Industrial Property, Nacional Financiera, Bancomext and the business accelerators of the federal government abroad.

Private institutions
The institute has worked closely with business organizations on diverse SME promotion projects in order to strengthen the incubation process of Tecnológico de Monterrey. An example of this can be seen in the collaboration projects carried out with Santander Bank, whose support made it possible to create the Emprendetec portal, create an incubation grant fund, institute the National Business Innovation Award and establish the Latin American University Business Incubator Network, comprising 12 universities.

The Technology Parks Strategy

The nature of technology parks
Technology parks have different names throughout the world. They are known as research parks, technology parks, science parks and innovation parks (Aguirre 2008). But they are all based on the premise of creating an environment that links business with knowledge. Stanford Research Park, created in 1951 at the initiative of that prestigious university, is considered the first technology park. It is estimated that there are now more than 400 technology parks in the world, the majority located in the United States, Western Europe and Asia.

The activities of technology parks depend significantly on their relationship to universities. They can be considered tools of the knowledge-based economic development models which, combined with other strategies, are intended to provoke changes in local economies. Jiang Zeming, the former president of China, considers them 'the most important invention of the technological industrialization of the 20th century'.

In general terms, a technology park can be defined as an infrastructure development which:

- incorporates centers of research and technological development with technology-based companies and services;
- has a high-quality physical environment and the atmosphere of a university campus to create a synergetic effect in the transfer and exchange of knowledge and the generation of new companies;
- is located within a university or research institute or within a reasonable distance of an institution of that type.

In this infrastructure several primary activities are carried out. They promote the growth of research, commercialization of technology and knowledge-based companies. They develop the wealth of the communities where the technology park is located through the promotion of the culture of innovation and the competitiveness of its associates and the knowledge-based institutions. And by doing so, they provoke an economic overspill into the community.

Background of Tecnológico de Monterrey technology parks strategy
Once the entrepreneurial and incubation activities reached a critical mass at Tecnológico de Monterrey system, another element was required to achieve the desired impact on the regional economies: a vision of the knowledge economy. According to the sequence of research, development, innovation and incubation, and based on successful experiences in prosperous economic regions, Tecnológico de Monterrey concluded that technology parks are highly useful instruments for increasing knowledge-based development.

Using successful models from one region of the world, however, does not necessarily guarantee success in another. Therefore after researching and analyzing the models used in other countries, Tecnológico de Monterrey developed an original strategy with models adapted to the idiosyncrasies of different regions of Mexico, to the characteristics of its enterprises, to the political reality and to the principles of Tecnológico de Monterrey itself. As a result, Tecnológico de Monterrey has determined the following strategic role for its technology parks:

- They should be efficient instruments for the transfer of technology as well as for the creation and attraction of enterprises of high added value.
- They should adjust to the models that capitalize on the knowledge generated by the universities and then transform it into social and economic wealth.
- They should become a fundamental element of local systems of innovation.

On the other hand, Tecnológico de Monterrey recognizes that there are diverse models for technology parks, each of which requires a strategic plan, infrastructure and a specialized model of administration. The selection of a technology park model depends greatly on the institutional resources where it will be established, on the alliances that are formed around it and on the strengths of the particular region.

The development program for technology parks aligns the vision of Tecnológico de Monterrey with regional needs. It has been formulated according to its impact on regional communities and governments, including the 32 campuses that the institution has in Mexico and the campuses of Universidad TecMilenio, which it sponsors. As will be explained later, one of the models for technology parks defined by Tecnológico de Monterrey is directed to Universidad TecMilenio because of the particular characteristics of its educational model.

Over the next five years (2010–14), Tecnológico de Monterrey will encourage the operation of more than 20 Mexican technology parks in the states of Aguascalientes, Chihuahua, Coahuila, Estado de Mexico, Jalisco, Morelia, Morelos, Nuevo León, San Luis Potosí, Sinaloa, Sonora, Tabasco and Tamaulipas, as well as in Mexico City in the Federal District.

The four technology parks models
After taking into consideration the environmental, economic, demographic, political and social characteristics of the diverse regions of the country, Tecnológico de Monterrey has defined four models of technology parks that reflect these regional differences and national conditions. These models are based on best practices observed in various countries of the world, but they have been carefully adapted to the Mexican reality.

Model I: technology parks for high-value employment These technology parks are designed to house enterprises that seek human resources for high-value activities but which do not require science or research. They can provide specialized talent to technology enterprises in a location close to the university. Immediate feedback from companies is necessary to enrich the educational model and improve the profile of the graduates.

Model II: technology parks for the attraction and development of enterprises These technology parks are mainly combinations of high-tech incubators to encourage start-ups and landing centers to accommodate foreign technology enterprises that want to set up operations in the region. Technology parks of this type strongly support consulting services, technology administration, networks and the specialized exchange of the R&D capacities between universities and businesses. These technology parks do not themselves include R&D activities, but they supply a group of highly trained technology managers and brokers for these areas.

Model III: technology parks for enterprises with scientific activities   This model is similar to the previous one but includes specialized laboratories designed to satisfy the needs of highly sophisticated enterprises in sectors such as biotechnology or nanotechnology, which require immediate continuous access to laboratories.

Model IV: Regional technology parks with different sponsors   This model of technology parks is the most widespread in the world. Technology parks of this type are built on great expanses of land and have an infrastructure similar to that of a university campus. They house diverse R&D centers, universities, enterprises and services, all sharing the same space and thus facilitating relationships among the various entities. Given the expense and scope of these parks, they usually develop in regional projects financed by governments. However Tecnológico de Monterrey also plans to participate in this model of technology parks.

Approach to the development of technology parks
Before creating a technology park and finding effective projects for any of the models defined in this section, developers need a clear reason to justify establishing it in a particular region. In the proposal by Tecnológico de Monterrey, technology parks allow the incorporation of activities related to incubation, acceleration, landing, technology development and association with the business sector. They act as business centers and provide networking with scientific and academic activities.

This proposal is congruent with the experience of technology parks throughout the world, which have shown the value of creating synergy among researchers and business executives and have facilitated the association of solid business leaders with young and new business entrepreneurs. All those who participate in these technology parks are directly or indirectly involved in a physical space that encourages their personal interaction.

The idea of technology parks is supported by the physical proximity of the diverse participants in the various sectors – business, academic and scientific – as well as investors who can find support services and stimulate creativity as they explore new business opportunities. Because of this, the selection of the participants in a technology park is very important, as is the design of its installations and surroundings.

The following activities should be integrated into a technology park of Tecnológico de Monterrey model:

- Landing: support for establishing technology-based enterprises from outside the region.
- Incubation: support for developing and consolidating new enterprises and stimulating the creation of highly innovative projects.
- Acceleration: support for ensuring that the enterprise model functions correctly and reaches its goals faster than it would outside a technology park.
- Technological development: support for the technological development of the businesses, which may range from access to scientific laboratories to the development of projects by experts.
- Academic and scientific activities: support for the association of enterprises with researchers to carry out projects in basic science, and with students of different levels to enrich their academic experience as they participate in a high-technology business environment. At the same time, the businesses can find high-quality human resources with great potential for development.

The projects of technology parks established at the campuses of Tecnológico de Monterrey should, without exception, include activities that lead to scientific and technological development. This is made possible by technology brokers who associate and conduct business activities in conjunction with laboratory and research centers on the campus sponsoring the technology park, or directly with the research centers and laboratories installed in the technology park. This condition is fundamental to ensure that technology parks contribute to the evolution of Tecnológico de Monterrey as a leader in research and enterprise development.

Examples of operating technology parks

Technology park TecMilenio, Las Torres campus (Model I) The Center for Excellence in Open Standards at TecMilenio, Las Torres campus, was inaugurated in 2005. The university received support from IBM, the federal government and the government of the State of Nuevo León. Technology park TecMilenio Las Torres, at the university of the same name, was thereby enabled to begin operations. This technology park, whose purpose is to provide information technology and human development services, houses the following businesses: Infosys, Grupo NASA, Sinapsys, Aleph 5, Intersoftware, Viva Aerobús and Crosshorizons. The technology park is also developing projects with IBM and Microsoft. Among these projects is the Microsoft Innovation Center, whose objective is the development of mission-critical applications and certifications.

Collaboration between companies in the technology park and the university has allowed upper management to participate in various academic events while also providing TecMilenio University students with the opportunity to carry out professional practice programs, to become members of a work team and to receive training in various tools for software development in programs specially organized for them.

Center for Innovation and Transfer of Technology (CIT2) of the Monterrey Campus (Model II)   The Center for Innovation and Transfer of Technology (CIT2) of the Monterrey campus of Tecnológico de Monterrey is an example of a Model II technology park whose function is to promote the development of companies based on technology, to facilitate the transfer of technology, to accelerate the commercialization of new technologies and to facilitate the adaptation of technology-based companies in global markets, particularly Latin America.

CIT2 began operations in 2005 with the mission of covering the following strategic areas: mechatronics and advanced manufacturing, information and communication technologies, software, design engineering and industrial design, and sustainable development. Since CIT2 is a Model II technology park of Tecnológico de Monterrey, it is physically a part of the operations that make up the incubators of technology-based enterprises. It is also the enterprise accelerator of the landing program, which houses foreign technology businesses that are looking to establish operations in the region and a commercialization program for the technology produced at Tecnológico de Monterrey using research by entrepreneurship students. Finally it includes networking activities and encourages links between park residents and local businesses, financial institutions and entrepreneurial organizations, among others. It acts as a true business center.

CIT2's mission is to increase greatly the establishment of high-technology enterprises in Nuevo León and to offer solutions related to business and regional competitiveness in technology administration and transfer. Among its specific, most important objectives are:

- to generate and attract high-tech businesses;
- to provide added value to businesses by means of knowledge transfer related to technology and commerce from Tecnológico de Monterrey and the region;
- to connect businesses to the ecosystems of regional and national innovation.

By the middle of 2008, CIT2 had succeeded in welcoming and adapting nine global technology corporations to the region and was instrumental in the growth of 15 local technology-based businesses. In addition the CIT2 had coordinated the start-up of seven projects between Tecnológico de Monterrey and its member companies. It had also participated in the creation of two spin-offs of businesses housed in CIT2 and in the generation of more than 130 high-paying jobs in the areas of software, telecommunications and engineering.

Center for Innovation and Strategic Product Development (CIDEP) of Tecnológico de Monterrey at PIIT Nuevo León State Research and Technological Innovation Park (Model IV) In 2003 the Nuevo Leon state government and the universities located in Monterrey, the state's capital, proposed moving the state toward a knowledge-based economy, for which they formulated the project Monterrey: International City of Knowledge, which would require mechanisms to attain the proposed objective.

Technology parks are one of the mechanisms that have had the greatest impact on the implementation of this type of economic transformation in other regions of the world. This success was the inspiration for creating the research and technological innovation park (PIIT). This park contributes to the generation and incorporation of high-tech or high-value-added companies, as well as to the repositioning of Monterrey's present-day industry.

To accomplish this, the PIIT would include in its facilities universities, research centers and companies that wanted to conduct knowledge-based activities like research, technological development and new product design. Construction of the PIIT began in 2006 on its 70-hectare (173-acre) site located in the northeast of the city of Monterrey, just a few hundred meters from Mariano Escobedo International Airport, with an investment of over 100 billion pesos by the state government.

Some of the centers that form part of the first phase of this technology park are:

- the Center for Innovation, Research and Development in Engineering and Technology, Universidad Autónoma de Nuevo León;
- the Engineering and Industrial Development Center, the National Board of Science and Technology and the federal government;
- the Center for Research in Advanced Materials, the National Board of Science and Technology and the federal government;
- the Center for Research and Advanced Studies, the National Board of Science and Technology and the federal government.

Tecnológico de Monterrey will be operating its CIDEP in the PIIT. CIDEP is one of the institution's most ambitious projects in terms of strategy and resources. The PIIT is based on an interdisciplinary integration and collaboration model between regional universities and the leading research centers in the country, and it has the support of the specialized infrastructure required for this type of technology park. Its mission is to capitalize on the different institutions' intellectual resources in order to stimulate the creation and growth of technology companies and thus trigger regional economic development.

The Center for Innovation and Strategic Product Development (CIDEP) of Tecnológico de Monterrey located at PIIT   The CIDEP, located in the research and technological innovation park, is central to the objectives of the project Monterrey: International City of Knowledge. With just over 10 000 square meters (107 640 square feet) of construction, the CIDEP is the first center that Tecnológico de Monterrey has developed on its part of the PIIT site. The CIDEP's specialized infrastructure has the capacity to house state-of-the-art laboratories, including rapid prototyping, network and electronics laboratories. The CIDEP is a strategic gateway for the talent of Tecnológico de Monterrey and a platform for association with global enterprises. The CIDEP targets companies that design, develop and engineer new technologies in information technologies and communications, software and electronics.

ENTREPRENEURSHIP ECOSYSTEM DEVELOPMENT

Initiation and Consolidation of the Entrepreneurship Program

Tecnológico de Monterrey has been offering its entrepreneurship program, which is designed to trigger an entrepreneurial spirit in students, for almost 30 years. At the end of the 1970s, the school decided that its graduates needed an entrepreneurial attitude rather than aiming to find a position in an existing company. To achieve this attitude, students required special preparation that would not only introduce them to this new field but also give them the tools they needed to follow this path. As a result Tecnológico de Monterrey established an entrepreneurship program in 1978 with a small group of professors and business people who guided students through the process of creating a business. This program, which later became the entrepreneurship program, stressed the preparation of entrepreneurs by complementing traditional professional studies with real-life experience during which students learned to generate and develop their entrepreneurial ideas.

After the first few years of this educational experiment, which was available as an elective to students, the entrepreneurship program was formally structured in September 1985 by making it a compulsory course on every campus and in all undergraduate curricula. The course was mainly practical and some of the required exercises eventually led to the creation of new companies.

A step forward: the entrepreneurship modality in the curricula
In order to have a greater impact on entrepreneurs, Tecnológico de Monterrey added the entrepreneurship modality as well as the international and internship modalities to the undergraduate curricula in January 2004. Students from any major could choose this educational complement if they were interested in starting a business while studying for their bachelor's degree at Tecnológico de Monterrey. Once they choose the entrepreneurship modality, students must choose either a new business approach, where they can create a new firm based on their own ideas, or a technology approach, where they can create a company based on technological developments generated by researchers at Tecnológico de Monterrey.

Both approaches make it possible to structure a business project that highlights innovation and the creation of value. The entrepreneurship modality involves completing workshops in addition to the undergraduate curriculum, which focus on competencies such as leadership, the use of creativity, innovation and the application of technology to create value, initiative and problem solving, and teamwork. Moreover while at the business incubator students take four courses oriented toward starting their own business.

The entrepreneurship modality seeks to strengthen undergraduates' entrepreneurial potential by offering them as a learning platform the creation and operation of a company using a practical, real-life approach, in contrast with the course called Entrepreneurial Development, which is compulsory for all Tecnológico de Monterrey undergraduates. It focuses on awakening an entrepreneurial spirit but does not require the creation of a company. Students who choose the entrepreneurship modality benefit from taking advantage of the service offered by Tecnológico de Monterrey's business incubators, which is a laboratory of the courses that make up the entrepreneurship modality.

Business Incubators: Where Business Ideas Come True

The innovations gradually introduced by Tecnológico de Monterrey in its academic programs develop an entrepreneurial spirit in its graduates while promoting business ideas. This led to the recognition of a need for a business incubation model that would make it possible to convert ideas developed in academic exercises into real companies. This is how the business incubators of Tecnológico de Monterrey began.

The first business incubator started operation in October 2001 at the Monterrey campus. Over the following years other campuses set up similar incubators. In the meantime, the institution structured an incubation model that incorporated the virtual business incubation modality in 2002 as a strategy to expand its services and the area of influence of business incubators.

The virtual modality led to the construction of the Emprendetec portal, which began operating in 2003. Thanks to the results rapidly achieved by this model and to its capacity to offer both face-to-face and virtual advisory services, the new Incubator Network of Tecnológico de Monterrey was certified in May 2004 by the Ministry of the Economy as a model that could be transferred to other organizations and institutions that wished to implement their own business incubators.

The importance of creating companies and the resulting generation of jobs led Tecnológico de Monterrey to include this activity in the document 'Vision and mission of Tecnológico de Monterrey towards the year 2015' (http://www.itesm.mx/2015/english/) in February 2005. This document states that by 2015, Tecnológico de Monterrey should be 'the leading educational institution in Latin America' in the 'generation of business management and incubation models'. In the text of this mission statement, Tecnológico de Monterrey undertakes to 'create, introduce and transfer incubator models and networks to contribute to the generation of companies'. This objective was expressed in the third strategy outlined by Tecnológico for fulfilling its mission.

The student and graduate profile, which forms part of the aforementioned document, establishes that one of their distinctive characteristics is their 'capacity for entrepreneurship and innovation'. As a result of these precise definitions, over the past three years (2006–08) Tecnológico de Monterrey has invested a great deal of effort in consolidating and diversifying activities related to entrepreneurship and the creation of new companies. This is evidenced by the 106 business incubators that currently work in the institution's network.

These incubators, their operational model, the types of companies they generate, the way in which the model is transferred to other institutions, their association with public and private institutions, and their orientation toward the future are all reported in this publication.

The business incubator network of Tecnológico de Monterrey today
The 106 business incubators that integrate the network of Tecnológico de Monterrey are operated by the 33 campuses, which means that some campuses run more than one incubator. The business incubator network

and its incubation model initially focused on intermediate-technology firms. Later on, however, the incubators had to offer incubation for technology-based firms and traditional micro companies that demand different support programs because of the nature of their business models. Although the incubation model is unique, it therefore incorporates distinctive components for each type of company.

The result is that the business incubator network of Tecnológico de Monterrey currently consists of three incubator subnetworks: one that incubates technology-based firms, another that serves intermediate-technology companies, and a third that gives advice to traditional micro companies. Note that for Tecnológico de Monterrey, social incubators are devoted to the development of the latter type of company. The business incubators of Tecnológico de Monterrey represent an integral platform for creating and developing new companies, and they also facilitate the tools and offer the resources required to provide entrepreneurs with more and better opportunities to start and expand their own businesses.

The business incubator network of Tecnológico de Monterrey supports students from all undergraduate majors and all postgraduate programs offered by Tecnológico de Monterrey. It also supports Tecnológico de Monterrey graduates and people from the external community.

The transfer model
Tecnológico de Monterrey first transferred its business incubation model in 2005. By doing so it began fulfilling its commitment to 'creating, implementing and transferring incubator models and networks to contribute to the generation of companies', as expressed in the mission statement. With these actions Tecnológico de Monterrey contributes to the development and well-being of society since the creation of new businesses entails the generation of new jobs.

The transfer model does not just include the transfer of vital processes that are necessary for the efficient operation of a business incubator; it also provides the institution in question with support in the real application of such processes during the first year of activities of the new incubator, the period covered in the transfer agreement entered into between Tecnológico de Monterrey and the interested institution. Tecnológico de Monterrey has transferred its business incubation model to 12 educational institutions and government agencies, all of which have evaluated the quality of the transferred model as excellent.

Operational Statistics of the Business Incubator Network of Tecnológico de Monterrey

The business incubator network of Tecnológico de Monterrey consists of three business incubator subnetworks that provide services for technology-based companies, intermediate-technology companies and traditional micro companies, respectively. Of the 106 business incubators that make up the business incubator network of Tecnológico de Monterrey, 8 incubate technology-based companies, 50 incubate intermediate technology companies, and 48 are social incubators.

The 106 business incubators distributed throughout the country currently serve more than 2000 companies, of which 1300 are in the initial stage of the incubation process, while the remaining 700 are already operational and in the growth stage. These companies are supported by 484 experts who act as guides in the different areas of business.

The companies in the incubation process have generated more than 6400 direct jobs. Twenty-three percent of the companies that participate in the incubation models are generated by students, 11 percent by Tecnológico de Monterrey graduates, and the remaining 66 percent by other entrepreneurs from the community.

Development of the Technology Parks Strategy

Origin of the strategy
Science and technology parks have been widely diffused, having been propelled by their impressive growth in many regions of the world and their striking role in the newest knowledge-based economic development models. Universities are acting as the promoters of these efforts. Although some Mexican states like Nuevo Leon, Jalisco and Baja California have initiated the planning of technology parks, it was Tecnológico de Monterrey that launched a pioneering experiment in 2004 by buying property adjacent to the Monterrey campus and transforming the space for companies willing to work in collaboration with the university. After years structuring a model to integrate other emerging companies and programs to facilitate networking and additional services for the tenant companies, the success stories became known, and the model was adopted by other campuses in the system.

Based on the successful network organization of the incubators, the technology parks are also using models based on best practices. International models and experiences have also been studied and analyzed, but the goal is to develop a model suited to Mexico's particularities. The strategy of Tecnológico de Monterrey has earned top marks, even from the Ministry of the Economy, which has committed to support more than 20 potential projects being planned in 2009. Nuevo Leon, the state where Tecnológico de Monterrey was born and where its larger campus is located, has been a key region for trying strategies and then disseminating the experiences that have flourished.

Some outcomes

There are 12 parks in operation and 17 being assessed and planned for the next five years (2010–14). Tecnológico de Monterrey Park initiatives have resulted in the establishment in the region of more than 58 global technology-based firms and the growth of 24 technology-based companies. By the beginning of 2009 the support services provided to these companies, including relocation, adaptation, recruitment and liaison/brokerage services, had been consolidated. Approximately 1800 jobs were created or sustained at the technology parks, all of them of higher added value, with employees earning above-average salaries in their communities.

Toward the Future

Business incubation

In 2010 Tecnológico de Monterrey will have a total of 183 business incubators, of which 13 will be incubators for technology-based companies and 70 for intermediate-technology firms; 100 will be social incubators. The incubation model of Tecnológico de Monterrey faces the challenge of consolidating itself in the future as a mechanism that facilitates not only the operation of the existing business incubator network, but also the management of new national and international networks by means of strategic alliances that enable knowledge links, experience and training, and the formation of an appropriate business environment for the creation of companies in a globalized setting.

The technology parks strategy

The technology parks strategy was initiated to generate mobilization for a better social and economic dynamic in several Mexican regions, all of them envisioning a knowledge-based economy. From 2005–08, 12 parks have been established, more than 58 firms enlisted and more than 1900 high-value jobs created within these parks. This is an impressive rate for a country with a developing economy. At least 12 more parks are being planned, and most of them should be in operation by 2012. Because the parks have acted as integrators of other enterprise development programs like incubation and acceleration, it is expected that the technology parks will integrate the current 106 incubators that Tecnológico de Monterrey runs in Mexico, ultimately creating a synergistic program that will multiply the number of technology-based firms and jobs in the country. As these models are improved by subsequent experiences, they should be transferred to other universities, not only in Mexico but to other regions with similar characteristics and aspirations.

SUMMARY OF MAJOR LESSONS LEARNED

For entrepreneurship to succeed, more is required than the existence of motivated entrepreneurs. Ecosystems are needed to ensure the survival and growth of new firms and to spread the benefits (job creation and wealth) to the social and economic environment, thus fostering a better regional economy. Moreover the importance of components of the ecosystem like innovation and academia is more evident if the new businesses are based on high-value products and services that require knowledge and high-caliber talent.

The Tecnólogico de Monterrey embarked on activities to promote entrepreneurship more than 25 years ago (prior to 1985). The subsequent establishment of incubators was a natural step in the logical sequence of enterprise development, and the success of both actions became evident as programs multiplied on other campus in Mexico. However, the need for other elements was also obvious, particularly when the emphasis of the programs was more on innovation and technology. What was needed was a wider context for this new breed of business. The challenge was met by technology parks, which emerged as the appropriate model for the next stage in the construction of an ecosystem. To prevent failure with this new strategy, models were designed to suit the Mexican context. Development models for technology parks take into account the regional context and the organizational capabilities of each region as factors in determining the size, reach and resources needed to start operating the technology parks.

Technology parks integrate the components of the ecosystems. They serve as a liaison with governments to facilitate public funding programs for companies and research organizations willing to commercialize technologies, and also as a liaison with angel and venture capital organizations. To fill one remaining gap in the ecosystem, Tecnológico de Monterrey has begun to implement a new strategy called investment clubs, which stimulate the venture capital culture in the communities.

Over the years we have learned the importance of increasing the efforts to consolidate the entrepreneurial ecosystem in which the university community (students, faculty, researchers and administration) actively participates. Entrepreneurship is not simply one option; rather it is an attitude that permeates every aspect of life.

Creating an entrepreneurial ecosystem is more than facilitating the physical spaces where entrepreneurs interact. Physical space is important, but the ecosystem must include a wide array of components: the alignment of institutional objectives; access to university resources like laboratories, researchers and knowledge transfer; and a market-driven orientation for research. Also required are the participation of the business community through business angel groups; the participation of venture capital firms; and the active participation of municipal, state and federal government in creating the necessary legal framework and assigning economic resources to job creation and the establishment of new companies.

Networking is equally important. Entrepreneurs should be able to access any resource they need no matter where it is located in the entrepreneurial ecosystem. This is the main function of the recently founded Entrepreneurship Development Institute where Tecnológico de Monterrey integrates the entrepreneurial activity from all its campuses under the coordination of one office.

The Entrepreneurship Development Institute is responsible for coordinating the following programs on all of the campuses of Tecnológico de Monterrey:

- entrepreneurial academic programs;
- business incubator network;
- business accelerator network;
- technology parks network;
- knowledge transfers offices;
- intellectual property centers;
- business angel clubs;
- funds procurement office;
- links to research centers and laboratories;
- networking with private and public programs focused on entrepreneurship.

Recommendations

1. Leadership and management should be absolutely convinced of the importance of developing entrepreneurial programs.
2. A university that advocates entrepreneurship as a core activity should also have a clear vision of its role and responsibility in the economic development of its region, rejecting the notion that the university is an isolated organization.

3. The participation of a triple-layered framework in the community is fundamental. The lack of any one participant would result in poor and incomplete results.
4. Eventually all the elements of the ecosystem should be developed. The existence of one or two is insufficient to achieve the long-term objective of economic prosperity.
5. Leadership and specialized management for the entrepreneurial programs, incubators and parks are extremely important.

REFERENCES

Aguirre, José Manuel (2008), 'Parques Tecnológicos: Herramientas de Desarrollo Regional', Instituto Tecnólogico y de Estudios Superiores de Monterrey, Monterrey, Mexico.

Bustani, Alberto, Eugenio García and Francisco J. Cantú (2006), 'Strategies for moving from a teaching university towards a teaching, research and entrepreneurial university: Tecnológico de Monterrey experience', Triple Helix Conference, Addis Ababa, Ethiopia.

Corona, Treviño L., J. Doutriaux and Sarfaz A. Mian (2006), *Building Knowledge Regions in North America: Emerging Technology Innovation Poles*, Cheltenham, UK and Northampton, MA, USA: Edward Elgar.

Curtin, Richard (2003), 'Creating more opportunities for young people using information and communications technology', World Summit on Information Societies, Geneva, Switzerland, 12–14 December.

European Commission (2002), 'Country Strategy Paper: Mexico 2002–2006', ec.europa.eu/external_relations/mexico/csp/02_06_en.pdf.

GEM (2006), 'Global Entrepreneurship Monitor: GEM 2006 summary results', http://www.gemconsortium.org/download.asp?fid=532.

Mittelstädt, Axel and Fabienne Cerri (2009), 'Fostering entrepreneurship for innovation', OECD Directorate for Science, Technology and Industry Working Paper 2008/5.

Molina, A., D. Romero and B. Ramírez (2008), 'Estrategias del I + D + i2 en el Tecnológico de Monterrey para Impulsar el Desarrollo Competitivo Regional de México', Congreso de Sistemas de Innovación para la Competitividad, Consejo de Ciencia y Tecnología del Estado de Guanajuato (CONCYTEG).

Torres, A., Karla Giordano and Rosalba Regalado (2007), 'Incubadoras: Un desarrollo Eficaz', Instituto Tecnológico y de Estudios Superiores de Monterrey, Monterrey, Mexico.

7. National University of Singapore

Yuen-Ping Ho, Annette Singh and Poh-Kam Wong

INTRODUCTION

In common with other newly industrialized economies in Asia, Singapore has been moving towards a knowledge-based strategy for economic development in recent years (Wong and Singh 2008). Policy makers have charted a course for Singapore's transition from an investment-driven economy to an innovation-driven economy, emphasizing the building of intellectual capital and its commercialization to create value and jobs. While the role of Singapore's universities in nurturing talent has always been recognized, increasing prominence has been given in recent years to their role in stimulating economic growth through industrially relevant research, technology commercialization, high-tech spin-offs, attraction of foreign talent and injecting an entrepreneurial mindset among their graduates. This chapter examines how the National University of Singapore (NUS), the leading university in Singapore, is changing its role in Singapore's national innovation system (NIS).

Singapore's case is of particular interest to other small, late-industrializing economies because of its status as a relatively small city-state, where the pressure for globalization and the pace of change towards a knowledge-based economy to sustain economic survival are particularly intense. As such the challenges that the university system faces are likely to be similar to those that other small late-industrializing economies will be faced with in the near future. In particular, the experience of Singapore is of interest in studying how the mission and governance of local universities in latecomer economies may need to be reformed towards an 'entrepreneurial university' model to enable such economies to catch up more quickly in the global innovation race.

THE SINGAPORE ECONOMY: SETTING CONTEXT

The primary focus of Singapore's national innovation system during its emerging knowledge-economy development phase is the creation and commercialization of knowledge protected by intellectual property (patented high-tech innovations and trademarked designs, proprietary specialized knowledge assets and processes, and copyrighted creative contents). However, in this shift towards a knowledge-based economy, Singapore needs to overcome four key transformational challenges. First it requires a shift of Singapore's capabilities in terms of using technology towards capabilities in creating technology. While Singapore's success in leveraging foreign multinational corporations (MNCs) in earlier development phases cannot be denied, one consequence is that the country's reliance on imported technology has to some extent crowded out the development of indigenous innovative ability. As Singapore moves increasingly towards a knowledge-based economy, it will need to achieve a more balanced national innovation system that emphasizes both the attraction of foreign MNCs to bring more innovative activities to Singapore as well as the development of local innovation capabilities through greater public investment in research and development (R&D).

A second transformational challenge is that Singapore lacks a sufficient number of highly skilled knowledge professionals, especially research scientists and engineers (RSEs). In some ways, this is to be expected given Singapore's small size and thus limited manpower pool. However it is a major constraint to the future development of its national innovation system, given the critical mass of science and technology manpower needed for its high-tech industrial drive, especially in the life sciences.

The third challenge is the lack of an entrepreneurial culture and mindset among Singaporeans. Again, this is somewhat to be expected in a stable, rapidly growing economy with secure, high-paying jobs available in MNCs. However it was exacerbated by a government policy that provided incentives for the best and brightest graduates from each year to work in public service and in the prevalent government-linked companies (GLCs). As a consequence, a culture that eschews risk and failure has developed over the years, and entrepreneurship has not generally been considered a viable career option (Wong et al., 2005).

The final challenge is that the innovation system in Singapore is characterized by a relatively underdeveloped technology commercialization ecosystem. First, there is a lack of private enterprises capable of using R&D from public research institutes or universities to develop product or process innovations in the marketplace. This lack is the result of the underdevelopment of local high-tech enterprises, which is in turn due to the heavy reliance on foreign MNCs in the past. At the same time, even though foreign firms are increasing their innovation activities in Singapore, they still tend to have weak linkages with the local innovation actors, and their propensity to license locally produced technologies is in a nascent stage (Wong and Ho 2007). Secondly, the venture ecosystem for supporting new start-ups is also weak. Unlike advanced high-tech hubs like Silicon Valley (Lee et al. 2000), Singapore's venture capital (VC) industry is still in its early development stage, and the established VC funds tend to focus on less risky later-stage financing. A critical mass of sophisticated business angel investors is also lacking, and the dense social networks of venture professionals, mentors and deal-making institutions (start-up law firms, serial entrepreneurs, and so on) that characterize places like Silicon Valley are non-existent. Consequently, even if the public sector were able to increase its R&D output significantly, the underdeveloped venture ecosystem would make it difficult for such innovations to be commercialized via spin-offs.

The Singapore government has made a concerted effort to shift its policy focus and overcome these four transformational challenges since the late 1990s. For example in a report of the Subcommittee on Entrepreneurship and Internationalization, part of the larger Economic Restructuring Committee (ERC) Report released in September 2002, six broad areas of policy change were recommended to make the Singapore economy more conducive to entrepreneurial development:

1. Culture: to influence the cultural values of Singaporeans towards entrepreneurship by providing students and working professionals with more opportunities to learn about entrepreneurship.
2. Capability building: to attract more entrepreneurial talents from overseas and encourage greater mobility of talents between the public and private sectors.
3. Conditions: to reduce government regulatory red tape and review the role of GLCs in the domestic economy.
4. Connectivity: to enhance the global connectivity of Singaporeans to the world.
5. Capital: to improve the access to capital of start-ups and small and medium-sized enterprises.
6. Catalyst role of government: to extend investment and tax incentives currently available for large MNCs to smaller enterprises as well (ERC 2002).

In the context of major public policy changes that would shift the Singaporean economy towards a knowledge economy, it is inevitable that attention has increasingly been paid to changing the role and function of higher education, given its pivotal role in the national innovation system. For example the government has announced the establishment of a fourth university that will have a strong technology focus and involve significant partnership with a leading US and Chinese university. The National Research Fund also explicitly set aside a pool of funding, the University Innovation Fund, in early 2009 to support university research commercialization activities, over and above its research funding.

THE CHANGING ROLE OF THE UNIVERSITY IN THE NIS: THE ENTREPRENEURIAL UNIVERSITY MODEL

As argued by Etzkowitz et al. (2000) and Etzkowitz (2003), universities around the world are increasingly shifting from their traditional primary role as educational providers and scientific knowledge creators to a more complex entrepreneurial university model that incorporates the commercialization of knowledge and active contribution to the development of private enterprises in the local and regional economy. As a result universities have become an increasingly important component of the national innovation system and thus need to operate within a triple-helix nexus that involves close interaction with government and private industry.

In the context of a small newly industrialized economy like Singapore, Wong et al. (2007) suggest that the local university system should take on an additional economic role: attracting foreign talent. Given the small local population, Singapore needs to be able to tap first-class foreign talent to help staff the top echelons of specialized knowledge workers required for a knowledge economy. The experience of regions like Silicon Valley, Boston and London strongly suggests that the competition for global talent works not only through the increasingly globalized market for qualified technical professional specialists, but actually starts before the talent reaches the labor market, when top students are attracted from overseas. Many of those who return to their home countries continue to build economic links with the regions where they went to school and indirectly contribute to the vibrancy of those regions. This kind of brain circulation dynamic was well documented by Saxenian (2000, 2002) in the context of Silicon Valley and its growing links with Asia.

Wong et al. (2007) also emphasize that entrepreneurship plays a significant role in the content of university-wide education at entrepreneurial universities in late-comer economies. In particular, they argue that the university needs not only to take on new functions, but that the core function of education also needs to be reoriented. The need for the university to play an active role in fostering a more entrepreneurial mindset among students is arguably even more imperative in the context of Singapore, where the highly educated population has demonstrated a relatively low entrepreneurial propensity (Wong et al. 2005) because consistently high economic growth in the past generated relatively full employment and bright career prospects in the corporate (mainly MNC subsidiaries) and public sectors. With stable job opportunities and steady corporate careers no longer guaranteed in the competitive global economy of the new millennium, the university sector in Singapore urgently needs to reorientate student expectations of the job market and to prepare them for a more entrepreneurial world.

How has the university educational system in Singapore responded to the transformational challenges of Singapore's national innovation system since the late 1990s? To what extent has it moved towards the entrepreneurial university model as advocated by Etzkowitz, and in what ways has it incorporated the additional roles of attracting foreign talents and nurturing entrepreneurship in its core educational and research missions as advocated by Wong et al. (2007)? In the remainder of this chapter, we will examine the strategic changes made by NUS in pursuit of an entrepreneurial university model.

OVERVIEW OF NUS AND ITS TRANSITION TOWARD AN ENTREPRENEURIAL UNIVERSITY MODEL

Established in 1905, NUS is the oldest and largest public university in Singapore and the only one with the status of a Doctoral Research University-Extensive according to the Carnegie Classification of Institutes of Higher Learning because of the breadth of its faculty and the depth of its research output. Table 7.1 provides a profile of NUS in fiscal year (FY) 2007–08. With a teaching faculty of over 2100 and a student population of over 30 000, NUS is among the largest universities in Asia. It has an annual R&D budget of about S$366 million, which means that NUS constitutes about 8 percent of total R&D spending in Singapore. NUS is also the fourth-largest US patent holder in Singapore with 244 US patents granted as of 2008.

IMPETUS FOR CHANGE

Like most other public universities developed under the British Commonwealth tradition, the primary mission of NUS had been teaching,

*Table 7.1   Profile of National University of Singapore, fiscal year
2007–08*

Indicator	FY 2007–08
Faculty members	2 103
Research staff	1 710
Undergraduate students enrolled	23 330
Graduate students enrolled	7 020
Total research funding	S$366 million
Total number of research projects funded	1 775
Journal publications in SCI-Expanded/SSCI/A&HCI (calendar year 2008)	3 314
Patents filed	126
Patents granted	49
Cumulative number of US patents granted (calendar years 1990–2008)	244
Cumulative journal publications in SCI/SSCI/AHI (January 1998–October 2008)	29 113

Sources: NUS Research Report 2007–2008; NUS Annual Report 2008; USPTO Database
of Issued Patents; ISI – Essential Science Indicators.

with research as a secondary mission (Etzkowitz et al. 2000). While the 1980s and 1990s saw an increasing emphasis on research, mirroring the steady shift in the Singapore economy towards R&D (Wong 2006), it was not until the mid-1990s that NUS began to establish a technology licensing office. Even then patenting activities were relatively low (only 21 US patents granted cumulatively up to 1997), and the involvement of professors and students in spinning-off companies was relatively rare before 2000.

The major impetus for more rapid growth in technology commercialization activities came only in the late 1990s, partly precipitated by the Asian financial crisis of 1997 that caused a recession in the Singaporean economy the following year. A major economic restructuring strategy was formulated by the government in response (ERC 2002) that highlighted the need to accelerate the shift towards an innovation-driven, knowledge-based economy and recognized the impetus for the local university to play a greater role in technology commercialization.

The impetus for change from the outside environment coincided with the imminent retirement of the vice-chancellor of NUS, which provided an opportunity for the government to effect change at NUS at a much faster pace by bringing in an external candidate for the top leadership role at NUS (now called 'president' to reflect the shift towards the US university model as the global benchmark). Singapore born and United States trained, the new president, C.F. Shih, came to NUS with strong credentials, having worked at a leading US corporation (General Electric) and having held a research leadership role in a major research lab at an Ivy League university (Brown University) in the United States. With strong government support, Shih provided the crucial leadership to accelerate significantly the pace of change of several initiatives that were already in motion, but more importantly he initiated a strategic shift towards embracing an entrepreneurial university model. As is typical of visionary leaders, he did this by establishing a new strategic vision for the university that encompassed an explicit recognition of entrepreneurial development, and by creating a new organizational vehicle to spearhead the change to the new vision.

SETTING STRATEGIC DIRECTION FOR CHANGE: THE 'GLOBAL KNOWLEDGE ENTERPRISE' VISION

As part of his strategy to set NUS on a new direction for development, President Shih articulated a vision for the university: to become a global knowledge enterprise. This vision signaled two strategic dimensions for change: first the need for NUS to compete in the global arena rather than the national economy, and second the need to add a more entrepreneurial aspect to NUS's research and educational activities, particularly in terms of accelerating the commercialization of the university's knowledge and producing more entrepreneurial-minded graduates. These two dimensions – more global competition and more entrepreneurial research and education – are closely intertwined, giving rise to both synergy and tension. On the one hand, since the domestic market of Singapore is small, success in knowledge commercialization requires the mindset and the skills to compete globally; hence entrepreneurial development activities must have a global orientation. On the other hand, the overall drive towards academic excellence at a global level also exerts significant constraints on what can be done on the entrepreneurial dimension. In other words, the pursuit of entrepreneurial activities cannot be at the expense of achieving global excellence in research and education. From a political perspective, the vision statement reassured the faculty and government that NUS would make pursuing global academic excellence a priority while allowing room for new initiatives toward entrepreneurship to be explored.

A major development in the drive to become globally competitive was a shift away from local manpower development towards the objective of making the university a global educational hub that attracts top foreign students and faculty in increasing competition with other leading universities in the world. In line with this globalization drive, NUS also began revising faculty compensation and policy, making it more flexible so that the university could pay more to attract top faculty and also reduce the pay of underperforming faculty. Tenure and promotion policy was made much more stringent and performance-based in line with leading universities in the United States. Enrollment of foreign students also increased, while more local students were encouraged to go on exchange programs abroad for at least a semester to gain international exposure.

To give NUS the necessary institutional flexibility to become globally competitive, the Singapore government allowed NUS to become corporatized in 2006. Although public funding support remains significant, with clear strategic goals to be achieved every three to five years, NUS was given much greater autonomy in how to achieve its targeted outcomes. Moreover NUS was encouraged to aim high after corporatization, with the government indicating that it was willing to commit to greater funding if the chances of achievement were realistic. Indeed when the *Times Higher Education Supplement* introduced the annual global ranking of universities in 2004, which showed NUS overall within or close to the top 20 in the world, the president's commitment to the strategic vision of differentiating NUS as an entrepreneurial university was reinforced, and the Singapore government appears to have strongly endorsed a more significant role and contribution by NUS towards the entrepreneurial development of Singapore.

ORGANIZATIONAL STRATEGY: THE CREATION OF NUS ENTERPRISE

Complementing his vision statement, President Shih created a new division in the university to spearhead the pursuit of activities to make NUS entrepreneurial. He also hand-picked a professor from the engineering school, Jacob Phang, who had been one of the first to start a venture to commercialize his inventions, as the first chief executive officer (CEO) of the new organization. Under the broad mission of injecting a more entrepreneurial dimension to NUS's education and research, Phang was tasked to make NUS Enterprise the primary organizational vehicle for coordinating and managing all major university activities related to technology commercialization and entrepreneurship promotion within NUS. As there were already some existing units within the university that were related to that broad mission, the new CEO was asked to take them under his wing and restructure them as he saw fit, and he was otherwise given great latitude to define and implement new initiatives that would make the university 'more enterprising'. To launch the new division, an annual operating budget equivalent to about 1 percent of the university's overall budget was set aside.

The fact that the CEO of NUS Enterprise would report directly to the university president and have a broad mission was significant because it gave him a mandate to adopt an integrated, coordinated approach in performing the generic technology commercialization roles of an entrepreneurial university. An integrated approach was indeed taken by the CEO who, after some early experimentation, assembled and incorporated seven major operating units in the new NUS Enterprise cluster by 2004. In early 2006 Phang, the original CEO, decided to relinquish his position so that he could devote himself full-time to growing the high-tech venture he had founded before becoming CEO. A new CEO, Lily Chan, was recruited from outside NUS. She had significant prior technology commercialization experience, having been a biomedical researcher and also having run a biomedical start-up. She later joined the Economic Development Board to promote biomedical investment in Singapore, before becoming a key member of the team running BioOne, a S$1 billion VC fund set up by the government to invest in life science start-ups. Building upon what had been accomplished up to then, Dr. Chan streamlined the various operating units into five as shown in Table 7.2.

The five units can be divided into two main groups. The first group

Table 7.2   Functional units in NUS Enterprise, 2008

Units of NUS enterprise in 2008	Core functions
NUS Entrepreneurship Centre (NEC)	• Experiential entrepreneurship education • Outreach • Entrepreneurship research • Entrepreneurship support services, including seed funding of NUS-related start-ups, enterprise incubation and mentorship programs
Industry Liaison Office (ILO)	• Technology licensing and IP management • Industrial liaison
NUS Overseas College (NOC)	• Overseas high-tech start-up internship with education program
NUS Extension (NEX)	• Continuing education
NUS Publishing (NUP)	• University press

comprises the NUS Entrepreneurship Centre (NEC), the Industry Liaison Office (ILO) and the NUS Overseas College (NOC). The second group comprises NUS Extension (NEX) and NUS Publishing (NUP), which are incorporated as independent corporate entities and operate as relatively autonomous businesses. We will focus our discussion on the first group of operating units since they are integral to NUS Enterprise's core mission of facilitating university technology commercialization, as opposed to the second group, which is somewhat peripheral. While many of the functions performed by these three core operating units are conventional and could be found in many universities, what distinguish the NUS Enterprise model are: (1) its effort in coordinating and creating synergies across functions; and (2) its entrepreneurial approach in spawning a number of new initiatives that represent significant innovations for NUS. We highlight below a number of these new initiatives.

KEY INNOVATIVE PROGRAMS OF NUS ENTERPRISE

Entrepreneurship Education Initiatives of the NUS Entrepreneurship Centre (NEC)

NEC was established in NUS Enterprise with the aim of promoting entrepreneurial learning in the NUS community through experiential educational programs and various outreach activities, to provide entrepreneurship support services to NUS professors, students and alumni wanting to start their own ventures, and to advance knowledge in the policy and practice of technology venturing in Singapore and the region through research. It was originally established in 1988 as a university-level centre called the Centre for Management of Innovation and Technopreneurship (CMIT). In 2001, it became a division of NUS Enterprise and was renamed the NUS Entrepreneurship Centre.

Like entrepreneurship centres established in many universities, NEC offered a wide range of educational programs, both within the classroom and outside. What distinguished NEC's non-classroom educational activities was an explicit attempt to reach beyond the campus to help evangelize and catalyze the development of the external venture ecosystem, and to make NUS into a magnet for entrepreneurial networking activities that link the NUS community with the external venture ecosystem. As highlighted earlier, this venture ecosystem catalysis role was important because the external venture ecosystem was still relatively underdeveloped in Singapore. For example, NEC pioneered the national business plan competition, Startup@Singapore, in Singapore in 1999. Although the competition drew its initial inspiration from the MIT S$50K competition, NEC opted to open its competition to the entire Singapore community rather than NUS students only. The director of the centre also helped found and chaired a business angel group, the Business Angel Network Southeast Asia (BANSEA) in Singapore. It operated like the Band of Angels in Silicon Valley, thereby helping to plug NUS into the nascent angel investment community in Singapore.

Another distinctive approach adopted by NEC was to launch a Technopreneurship minor program open to all NUS undergraduates, but with a strong focus on students in science and engineering. The goal was to make students in technical disciplines more business savvy and entrepreneurial-minded, which helped address a weakness in the existing programs at NUS, where students in technical disciplines had few opportunities to learn entrepreneurial skills. Interestingly NUS Enterprise initially asked the business school at NUS to offer these courses to technical students, but the business school declined because it was uncertain whether the demand would last. Although NEC was not an academic department, thanks to the strong championing of NUS Enterprise it was granted a special academic teaching unit status by the provost to mount the courses. Through an active marketing program that leveraged the centre's various non-classroom educational activities, NEC was able to increase enrollment rapidly in its technopreneurship courses from fewer than 200 in the first year to over 1300 by 2005–06. Once NEC was established as a viable program, its administration was transferred to the NUS Business School in 2007. NEC subsequently launched a new entrepreneurship learning program called Innovative Local Enterprise Achiever Development (iLEAD) that offers a seven-month internship opportunity in selected local high-tech start-ups for NUS undergraduates, followed by a two-week overseas study visit to Silicon Valley or China.

Another function of NEC was to provide targeted assistance to NUS spin-offs. Because of the relative underdevelopment of the venture ecosystem, academic entrepreneurs who wanted to spin off their own ventures faced a daunting prospect. Thus one of NUS Enterprise's first acts was to establish an NUS Venture Support (NVS) Division that offered incubator facilities on campus to give physical infrastructure support as well as selected advisory services to NUS-related start-ups. However the NEC leadership team quickly recognized that this was not enough. Through the active championing of the CEO, NUS Enterprise was able to convince NUS senior management to provide an allocation of S$5 million (in two tranches) to establish a seed-funding scheme, the NUS Venture Support Fund (NVSF), for very early-stage seed funding of up to S$300000 to promising NUS spin-off companies led by NUS staff, students and alumni. The aim was to incubate university-connected new ventures so they would become viable candidates for external funding by venture capitalists, angel investors or corporate investors, or until they achieved significant organic growth. Secondarily this activity reinforced the goal of making NUS the entrepreneurship ecosystem hub for the region. Between 2004 and the end of 2006, NVSF funded a total of 11 NUS start-ups out of over 40 that applied.

A separate student start-up fund known as the Fund for University Student Entrepreneurs (FUSE) was established in 2005 to provide developmental funding to new ventures started by students or recent graduates. A total of 21 student start-ups were funded under FUSE by the end of 2006.

Co-funding for these two schemes has been obtained from two public sources: SPRING SEEDS, a government scheme that provides one-to-one matching funds for NVSF (capped at S$300 000), and the SPRING Entrepreneurial Talent Development Fund (ETDF), another scheme targeted at student entrepreneurs that provides three-to-one matching funds for FUSE (capped at S$45 000 per company). Although NVS was initially established as a separate unit from NEC, it received close advisory and management support from NEC, including the formation of the investment committee. After the new CEO came onboard in 2006, NVS was merged into NEC as part of the overall organizational streamlining. Besides expanding the physical incubation services, NEC also initiated a mentorship program that brought experienced entrepreneurs, investors and senior executives to campus to provide regular coaching to NUS spin-off companies. A number of technology-specific seed funding schemes were also introduced, including one for interactive digital media and another for clean technology. NEC has also developed programs to assist NUS professors and students in applying for various new government grant schemes that have been launched in recent years to support university technology commercialization, such as the SPRING Proof of Concept (POC) and Proof of Value (POV) grants.

The NUS Overseas College (NOC) Program

The NOC program was introduced by NUS Enterprise in 2001 as an initiative that integrates globalism and entrepreneurship. Originally conceived by the university president, the basic concept of NOC was to send the brightest and most entrepreneurial-minded NUS undergraduates to entrepreneurial hubs around the world to work as interns in high-tech start-up companies for one year, during which time they would also take courses related to entrepreneurship at partner universities. In essence, the NOC program represented an experiment in learning entrepreneurship by immersion, that is, by immersing students as apprentices in a high-tech start-up or growth enterprise in a foreign location to expose them to the tacit aspects of entrepreneurial practice and foreign business culture. The program was conceived as a long-term investment in cultivating a global mindset and network connections in future entrepreneurial leaders. As such, it was not expected that the students would start their own ventures right after graduation, but rather that they would be infused with an entrepreneurial mindset that would orient their future research towards commercializable innovations and influence their future career choices towards more entrepreneurial and innovative pursuits. The program also aimed to help them establish valuable lifelong social networks within the entrepreneurial communities of high-tech hotspots overseas, so that they would be more inclined towards, and better equipped for, working in or starting high-tech start-ups with global aspirations.

The first NOC program was launched in Silicon Valley in 2002, followed by Philadelphia in 2003, Shanghai in 2004, Stockholm in 2005, Bangalore in 2006 and Beijing in 2009. The program aimed to accommodate a total of 200 to 250 students per year. NUS Entrepreneurship Centre worked closely with NOC to provide educational support to this overseas internship program by helping develop academic collaborations with the selected partner universities overseas (for example Stanford in Silicon Valley, Fudan in Shanghai, the Royal Institute of Technology – KTH – in Stockholm and Tsinghua University in Beijing), and by conducting additional entrepreneurship courses unavailable from the partner universities while also providing academic supervision of internship-based student projects.

The above description shows that by using the organizational mechanism of NUS Enterprise NUS was able to launch the NOC program in a relatively short time, cutting through red tape that would have otherwise ensnarled the program in faculty-level committees. The strong sponsorship of the president, who emphasized that NOC would be the flagship program that gave NUS high visibility in supporting entrepreneurship education, coupled with the entrepreneurial drive of the NUS Enterprise CEO, helped speed up the approval process. The close cooperation between NEC and NOC also helped ensure the smooth coordination and compatibility of academic course content between NOC and the Technopreneurship minor program.

Despite the high cost of the program (NUS gives substantial subsidies to each NOC participant), NOC appears to have achieved its objective of making the overall NUS Enterprise initiative highly visible not only in the local media but also internationally. An increasing number of NOC participants who have completed the program and returned to NUS are full of praise and appreciation for the transformational impacts of the program. Their word-of-mouth marketing is spreading through the Singaporean student communities, which raises the profile of NUS as an entrepreneurial university and attracts the more entrepreneurial-minded high school students to apply to NUS. Since a significant proportion of NOC participants are from other Asian countries, this visibility is likely to spread to the student communities in these countries as well.

Restructuring of Technology Licensing Functions

The technology transfer office at NUS was established in 1992 to handle technology transfer as part of the Industrial and Technology Relations Office (INTRO), including protecting and licensing NUS intellectual property (IP), and advising industry, faculty and staff on matters relating to IP. Initially the office was not perceived as a major source of assistance by either NUS inventors or industries seeking IP for licensing, since it did not have a full complement of experienced IP professionals. A number of instances were reported of the office making tough demands in terms of extracting licensing fees. For these reasons one of the first acts of the CEO of NUS Enterprise upon taking over INTRO was to enact some major initiatives to make the office more inventor-friendly, with less emphasis on maximizing licensing revenue and more emphasis on better and faster deployment of NUS technology to the marketplace, whether through licensing to existing firms or spinning off new firms. NUS Enterprise also created a policy of taking equity in lieu of royalty payments and of simplifying the process of negotiation on equity valuation for start-ups by NUS professors and students. INTRO was renamed Industry Liaison Office (ILO) in 2006 and reorganized to facilitate greater synergy between university–industry research collaboration and technology transfer facilitation. The professional staffing of the office was strengthened, and a more proactive approach was implemented to map out areas of technological strengths at the university so as to guide future innovation directions and to facilitate patent portfolio aggregation to achieve a critical mass in selected technology areas.

When they are considered in their entirety, the strategic initiatives described separately above have made NUS an emerging hub of an entrepreneurship ecosystem striving to improve entrepreneurship education and stimulate new venture creation in Singapore. Educational programs, incubation facilities, seed funding, mentoring programs and extensive social network generation have all combined to build a vibrant entrepreneurship community with NUS as the driving and nurturing force.

EVOLUTION OF THE ON-CAMPUS ECOSYSTEM: NEXT STAGE

Reflecting the entrepreneurial orientation of the founding CEO, the first three to four years of NUS Enterprise was rather fluid and fast-paced, at times even chaotic as the organizational leadership emphasized action rather than well-thought-out standard operating procedures and management systems. By empowering operating unit directors with strong ideas to champion them, this entrepreneurial organizational culture facilitated the rapid introduction of a number of innovative programs that were described earlier. In common with all entrepreneurial organizations, however, there was a tendency to undertake too many initiatives without enough systems and controls in place to ensure timely documentation and consistent application of management policy.

The departure of the first CEO in early 2006 was an opportune time for the university president to bring in a new leader, Lily Chan, to help manage the transition of NUS Enterprise to a more mature and stable organization. With a strong track record in managing venture capital investment and a prior background in running a biotech start-up, the new CEO quickly put in place a more balanced organizational development approach with a stronger emphasis on management systems. Reaffirming the integrated NUS Enterprise approach, she has emphasized the need for greater coordination and cooperation among the units of NUS Enterprise by consolidating some of the separate units, for example absorbing the Venture Support function into the NUS Entrepreneurship Centre, reorganizing INTRO into the Industry Liaison Office (ILO), and institutionalizing cooperative activities across the different operating units, rather than leaving it up to the initiative of their directors. She has also pushed ILO and NEC to take a more proactive approach in seeking out inventive and entrepreneurial-minded faculty members rather than waiting for them to apply. The strategic goals of NUS Enterprise have also been refined over time to focus on two core missions: embedding entrepreneurial learning as an integral part of an NUS education by providing experiential entrepreneurial education; and translating NUS's research into innovation and commercialization by providing industry partnership and entrepreneurship support.

Using these two strategic thrusts, the ultimate aim of NUS Enterprise is to help NUS achieve its goal of becoming a global knowledge enterprise

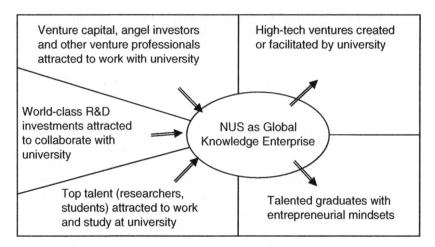

Figure 7.1   Vision of NUS's pivotal role in Singapore's knowledge economy

and playing a pivotal role in Singapore's knowledge economy (Figure 7.1) by attracting and transforming the relevant innovative resources into entrepreneurial output.

In summary, notwithstanding organizational changes, leadership transition and strategy evolution, it is fair to say that NUS has persevered in pursuing an integrated, coordinated approach to promoting technology commercialization and academic entrepreneurship through the organizational vehicle of NUS Enterprise. NUS Enterprise is autonomous from the conventional administrative and academic departments and reports to the university president through a high-level entrepreneurship committee that he co-chairs. Despite a change in the university presidency in 2008, NUS Enterprise has continued to receive sustained support from the senior management of NUS.

IMPACT OF NUS'S SHIFT TOWARDS THE ENTREPRENEURIAL UNIVERSITY MODEL

Overview

Because the shift towards the entrepreneurial university model is still at an early stage, it may be premature to assess the impact it will have on the university's performance in terms of the broader objectives that the new model implies. It is also not clear what performance benchmarks are

Table 7.3   Profile of changes in NUS before and after shift to entrepreneurial university model

Indicator	1996–97 academic year (AY)	2007–08 fiscal year (FY)
Teaching staff	1 414	2 103
% foreign	39.0	51.9[1]
Research staff	843	1 710
% percent foreign	70.1	78.6[1]
Undergraduate students enrolled	17 960	23 330
Graduate students enrolled	4 478	7 020
Graduate students as % of total student enrolment	20.0	23.1
% of foreign students studying at NUS	13[2]	34.6
Total research funding	S$102 million	S$366 million
Total number of research projects funded	1 751	1 759[3]
Journal publications in SCI/SSCI	1 307[4]	3 270[5]
Patents filed	13	96
Patents granted	4	30
Total patents granted by USPTO	21[6]	244[7]
Total spin-offs using NUS IP	6[6]	44[7]

Notes:
[1] % for FY 2004.
[2] % of total student intake for 1997–98.
[3] Figure for FY 2005.
[4] Calendar year (CY) 1996.
[5] CY 2008.
[6] CY 1990–97.
[7] CY 1990–2008.

Sources: NUS Research Report (various years); *NUS Annual Report* (various years); USPTO Database of Issued Patents; ISI Web of Science; NUS Office of Research.

appropriate for conducting such an assessment. Changes in performance in recent years may have been caused by factors other than those that we have associated with the shift towards the entrepreneurial university model. The above caveat notwithstanding, in this section we will examine the available empirical evidence on how NUS's technology commercialization performance has changed since the shift towards the Global Knowledge Enterprise model began.

Table 7.3 is an overview of the key changes NUS has undergone between 1996–97 and 2007–08. It shows that NUS has not only achieved considerable progress along the conventional performance dimensions of education and research output, but also that the university has performed even better in the new dimensions of foreign talent attraction, entrepreneurship promotion and technology commercialization. These are further elaborated below.

DEVELOPMENT AND ATTRACTION OF FOREIGN TALENT

An important part of the growth in Singapore's manpower – both students and faculty researchers – over the ten years 1998–2008 can be attributed to the ability of NUS to attract foreign talent. As can be seen in Table 7.3, between academic year (AY) 1997–98 and fiscal year (FY) 2007–08, the proportion of foreign students in NUS's student population nearly tripled from 13 percent to 35 percent. Although less dramatic, a significant increase is also evident in the rising share of foreigners among faculty and research staff recruitment since 1997. The share of foreigners among faculty members increased from 39 percent in 1997 to over 50 percent by 2005, while the foreigners' share among researchers increased from 70 percent to almost 80 percent. The biggest source of foreign researchers was mainland China, the source of over half of all foreign researchers by 2005.

KNOWLEDGE CREATION THROUGH RESEARCH PUBLICATIONS

The number of NUS research publications, as measured by internationally refereed publications covered by Thomson ISI's SCI-Expanded/SSCI/A&HCI (Science Citations Index Expanded/Social Sciences Citations Index/Arts and Humanities Citations Index), has grown fairly steadily over the years, from 1556 in 1997 to 3314 in 2008, an increase of 113 percent (see Table 7.4). More importantly the increase in quantity has been achieved along with a simultaneous improvement in quality as measured by the ratio of citations per publications. According to a study by the Higher Education Evaluation and Accreditation Council of Taiwan (HEEACT), NUS's global ranking in 2008 in terms of average citations per paper was 150 out of 499 universities ranked when analyzed over the previous 11 years, but it increases to 54 if analyzed over the past two years (2006–07) only (HEEACT 2008). Indeed the slowing of the rate of growth of the number of publications in recent years partly reflects a changing emphasis on quality over quantity of publications.

Table 7.4   NUS research publications, 1997–2008

Year	Journal articles covered by SSCI, A&HCI and SCI-Expanded
1997	1556
1998	1669
1999	1946
2000	2083
2001	2245
2002	2379
2003	2643
2004	2808
2005	3123
2006	3373
2007	3209
2008	3314

Sources: NUS Research Report (various years); ISI Web of Science.

KNOWLEDGE AND TECHNOLOGY COMMERCIALIZATION

In tandem with the growth in new knowledge creation between 1997 and 2007, the pace of new knowledge commercialization has also increased. These changes are analyzed under the topics of invention disclosure, patenting, licensing and industry collaborations, with a special focus on new ventures generated by university staff.

Invention Disclosures

The number of invention disclosures reported by NUS faculty and researchers from 1998 to 2006 has increased moderately, with the average number of disclosures reaching 97 per year over 2003–06 compared to 71 per year in the period 1998–2002 (NUS Industry Liaison Office; NUS (2005), *NUS Annual Report 2005*).

Patenting

NUS has played a significant role in Singapore's increased patenting activity over the ten years from 1997–2007. Since the early 1990s, NUS has implemented an intellectual property policy whereby all IP created

Table 7.5   Composition of NUS patents by technology category,
1990–2008

Technology category	Number of patents	%
Electrical and electronic	77	31.6
Computers and communications	58	23.8
Chemical	41	16.8
Drugs and medical	40	16.4
Mechanical	17	7.0
Other	11	4.5
Total	244	100.0

Source: Calculated from USPTO Database of Issued Patents.

by NUS staff is assigned to NUS, with ILO (then called the Industry and Technology Relations Office or INTRO) tasked to license the IP and distribute any return from commercialization equally among the inventor, the department and NUS central administration. The number of NUS patent applications was initially low but grew steadily from 1997 to 1999, averaging fewer than 80 per year for the period. The pace increased after 1999, with an average of just over 100 patents per year during the period 2000–2002, and 132 per year in 2003–07. The number of US patents granted has also increased since 1997. While the cumulative number of US patents granted to NUS was only 21 at the end of 1997, an average of 13 patents per year were granted in the period 1997–99, increasing to 24 per year over 2000–2002 and 30 per year over 2003–07 (*NUS Research Report* from various years; NUS Industry Liaison Office; *NUS Annual Report* from various years). These figures include patents filed in multiple countries.

The engineering faculty's dominance in NUS patenting is apparent from the technological fields in which the patents fall. Of the 244 US patents granted to NUS by the end of 2008, almost one-third were in the electrical and electronic technological category, with another 25 percent in computer technology and 17 percent in chemicals (see Table 7.5). Biomedical patents represent only 16 percent of all patents granted to NUS, a much lower proportion compared to many leading comprehensive universities in the world that have a medical school.

The patenting data also reveal an increase in collaborative innovation activities between NUS and external organizations in Singapore since 2000. From zero joint inventions with outside organizations before 1995, the proportion of joint inventions increased to 18 percent from 1995 to 1999, and further increased to 30 percent from 2000 onwards (see Table 7.6).

Table 7.6   Proportion of US patents invented by NUS in collaboration with external organizations

Year of grant	Proportion of patents jointly owned (%)
1990–94	0.0
1995–99	18.2
2000–04	29.3
2005–08	30.9
Total	27.5

Source: Calculated from USPTO Database of Issued Patents.

Licensing

Although the proportion of NUS inventions that were licensed out remains low, a clear increase in the volume of technology licensing activities since 2000 is evident from Table 7.7. As of the end of 2008, NUS had made 258 technology licensing agreements. Of these, fewer than one-quarter were issued before 2000; the bulk of licenses were signed in the nine years between 2000 and 2008. While it is true that the number of licensing deals concluded in the more recent period (2003–08) is lower than in 2000–2002, this is more a reflection of the changing policy of ILO, which focuses on a smaller amount of licensing that has a higher revenue potential, rather than targeting quantity regardless of revenue potential.

In terms of the amount of income generated from licensing, the total revenue from licensing has been on an upward trend since 1999, despite the reduction in the number of licensing deals more recently. Although the amount appears to be somewhat erratic from year to year, average licensing royalties have increased from an average of $83 800 per year before 2000 to nearly $290 000 from 2000 to 2002, and rose to $557 000 over 2003 to 2008 (see Table 7.8). As discussed earlier, ILO has been consciously pursuing a balanced approach to technology licensing in recent years, with priority given to promoting diffusion of university technology for its impact rather than to maximizing licensing income. To support academic spin-offs, ILO has also opted to take equity in lieu of royalties when licensing technology to spin-offs by academic inventors.

Industry Collaboration

Collaborative research projects with industry offer another avenue for translating university research into technology with commercialization

Table 7.7   NUS licensing agreements, 1987–2008

Year	Number	%
1987–96	29	11.2
1997–99	31	12.0
2000–02	124	48.1
2003–08	74	28.7
Total	258	100.0

Source: NUS ILO.

Table 7.8   NUS licensing royalties, 1996–2008

Time period	Total licensing royalties per year $'000	Average licensing royalties per year $'000
1996–99	335.0	83.8
2000–02	866.6	288.9
2003–08	3342.0	557.0

Source: NUS ILO.

Table 7.9   Research Collaboration Agreements (RCAs) at NUS: 1995–97 compared with 2005–07

Year	Number of RCAs	Number of RCAs with industry	% of RCAs with industry
1995	36	17	47.2
1996	30	13	43.3
1997	43	17	39.5
2005	129	35	27.1
2006	146	46	31.5
2007	119	39	32.8

Source: NUS ILO.

potential. As can be seen from Table 7.9, the number of research collaboration agreements (RCAs) undertaken by NUS has grown substantially over the last decade, rising from an average of 36 a year over 1995–97 to 131 over 2005–07. The absolute number of RCAs with industry has also increased, from an annual average of 16 over 1995–97 to 40 over 2005–07. Although the share of RCAs with industry has fallen over this time, it is

Table 7.10   Number of NUS spin-offs, 1980–2006

	Total number of spin-offs	Average number of spin-offs
1980–99	11	0.55
2000–02	15	5
2003–06	18	4.5
Total	44	1.6

Note: Includes one company which has been liquidated.

Source: NUS ILO and NUS Entrepreneurship Centre.

possible that this is due to the very small numbers of RCAs during the initial period. Aside from industry, RCAs have been formed with governmental bodies, public research institutes and foreign universities. In addition to forming RCAs, NUS also interacts with industry through consultancy contracts. Significant consultancy work has been undertaken by NUS faculty, averaging about 700 consultancies over 2003–04. However no reliable statistics are available in more recent years due to the decentralization of such data collection to individual faculties.

As mentioned earlier the limited ability of local firms to engage in knowledge commercialization means that universities in Singapore need to take a more direct role in commercializing their inventions by forming spin-offs. This commercialization model is different from that of the United States, for example, where technology licensing is emphasized more heavily (Heher 2006).

The effect of NUS's change of policy from 2000 on – encouraging technology commercialization through spin-offs and start-up formation – can be seen in Table 7.10. Of the 44 spin-offs (companies formed to commercialize NUS's patented inventions) created between 1980 and 2006, about three-quarters were established starting in 2000. The nature of the businesses is listed in Table 7.11.

In addition to the spin-offs that licensed IP from NUS, there also appears to have been an increase in the number of other start-ups by NUS professors, students and recent alumni since 2000. While no reliable statistics are available to track these start-ups, one gauge of their frequency post-2000 is the number of NUS-related start-ups that applied for various entrepreneurship support services offered by NEC, and the number of companies that actually received some form of support services from NEC (incubation, various grants and seed funding schemes). Between 2003 (when the incubation and seed funding programs were started) and 2008,

Table 7.11   NUS spin-off companies by nature of business

Nature of business	Number	%
Information technology	22	50.0
Biochemical	11	25.0
Electrical and electronics	3	6.8
Mechanical and machines	2	4.5
Scientific equipment	2	4.5
Other	4	9.1
Total	44	100.0

Source: NUS ILO.

it is estimated that about 51 companies received some form of funding support from NEC, and over 40 companies were incubated by the NUS Enterprise Incubator. Subtracting overlap among the two, there were more than 70 unique start-ups supported by NEC. The actual number of companies being considered for various support services by NEC was probably seven to eight times higher.

Since most of these NUS-related start-ups are quite recent, many are in the early stages of growth, and there have been no significant commercial successes as yet. It is encouraging to note, however, that more than ten of the companies supported by NEC have received follow-on investment by an external VC fund or angel investor. The combined annual revenue generated by these NUS-supported start-ups as of 2008 can be conservatively estimated as over S$12 million.

While it is difficult to gauge how much of the increased involvement in entrepreneurial activities by NUS professors and students since 2000 was facilitated by the various entrepreneurship education and support programs of NUS Enterprise, a number of indicators are instructive. Based on recent annual graduate employment surveys, graduates from various NOC programs appear to have exhibited three times the propensity to start their own business or to be employed in small start-up firms, compared to their peers. The number of participants in the annual StartUp@ Singapore business plan competition has also been steadily increasing over the years, with a growing number of the participating teams subsequently applying for seed funding or incubation at NUS.

In a limited time span, NUS's invention and commercialization activities have clearly increased in number and impact. As stated before, this activity was and is the major objective of Singapore's government to which NUS responded. With programs of entrepreneurship education, incubation and seed funding, mentoring and network building, all oriented towards the long run, NUS looks forward to continuing and increasing this trajectory of invention and new venture creation.

CONCLUSIONS AND LESSONS LEARNED

Our empirical analysis indicates that NUS's contribution to Singapore's national innovation system changed qualitatively in 2000. It shifted from being primarily a manpower provider and knowledge creator to taking on a more visible role in knowledge commercialization through increased patenting, licensing to private industry and spinning-off new ventures. Although the shift towards an entrepreneurial university model may not be the sole reason, the empirical evidence presented here is consistent with the hypothesis that universities need to adopt key elements of the entrepreneurial university model in order to contribute more effectively to the commercialization of university technology to private industry. While the specific governance model (for example the NUS Enterprise cluster approach) and initiatives and programs (for example the NOC program and the seed fund programs) that are adopted may apply only to the Singapore context, the reform experience of NUS may nonetheless be instructive for other East Asian universities seeking to develop their own entrepreneurial university model.

Given that the changes in innovation and commercialization performance have been quite recent, it is unclear whether they are sustainable over the long term. As of 2009, no outstanding success has been achieved in terms of major technological breakthroughs leading to licensing revenue or spin-offs leading to commercial success. While it is therefore by no means certain that NUS's shift towards the entrepreneurial university model will lead to significant economic pay-offs, we can take heart from the fact that some of the leading US universities also needed a long time to achieve commercial viability as measured by their technology licensing offices (Shane, 2004).

In addition to knowledge commercialization, our findings of a high and increasing level of recruitment of foreign students, researchers and faculty members by NUS are also consistent with the argument that an entrepreneurial university model for universities in small, open economies needs to incorporate the added task of attracting foreign talent. While the level of involvement by foreigners at NUS is probably exceptional by the standards of East Asian universities and perhaps even Western universities, it does suggest that the ability to compete for talent on a global scale is likely to be an important feature of any entrepreneurial university model for newly industrializing economies.

Last but not least, NUS's experiment in injecting a more entrepreneurial dimension to the educational experience of its students, particularly those in technical fields, may be instructive for universities facing the challenge of producing more business-savvy and entrepreneurial-minded technical graduates. The conventional solution of concentrating on technical specialization and leaving business skills and entrepreneurial acumen for a later stage (for example an MBA degree) may not be optimal for the increasingly dynamic marketplace in a global, knowledge-based economy, where creativity, an entrepreneurial mindset, social skills and international networking are increasingly important.

Several important lessons can be learned from the experience of NUS to date. In a small country, connection with the government and alignment of strategies is critical. If the government of Singapore had not focused on innovation and commercialization, NUS's chances to focus on entrepreneurship would have been greatly diminished. The belief of university leadership in the importance of entrepreneurship not only as an endeavour but also as an organizing model was important in connecting the school and government and developing a long-run strategy. Organizing all the entrepreneurship activities under one champion who combined new venture creation and educational expertise was an important first step towards creating mass and validity for the emerging entrepreneurship strategy. A crucial juncture occurs in the development of an entrepreneurship ecosystem when leadership must shift focus to include organizing and possibly reining in entrepreneurial efforts by consolidating gains and jettisoning unsuccessful ventures. It can be a tricky balancing act to impose organization while maintaining a spirit of entrepreneurship. A last requirement for success is that the university must expand beyond its walls to stimulate regional entrepreneurship education and activity. This expansion strengthens the university's position as an entrepreneurship ecosystem hub as it acts as an increasing magnetic force for all types of entrepreneurship activity: invention, new ventures, seed funding, later-stage funding, mentoring and ultimately a vibrant social network.

In conclusion, the case of NUS in Singapore illustrates an attempt by a university located in a small, newly industrialized economy to transform itself and thereby contribute more effectively to the dynamic shift of the country towards a regional knowledge-based economic hub. The approach adopted is admittedly risky: making technology commercialization and academic entrepreneurship an explicit goal of the university invites inevitable public and international scrutiny of the actual performance of the university in commercializing technologies. Given that many leading universities in the world have not yet been successful in promoting technology commercialization, the risk that NUS will fail to meet raised public expectations is significant. Moreover the pursuit of technology commercialization and academic entrepreneurship as an objective of the university requires extensive organizational change that will encounter considerable resistance. These risks are nonetheless worth taking, for the rewards of success are substantial.

REFERENCES

Economic Review Committee (ERC) (2002), *Report of the Entrepreneurship and Internationalisation Subcommittee*, Singapore: Ministry of Trade and Industry.

Etzkowitz, Henry (2003), 'Innovation in innovation: the Triple Helix of university–industry–government relations', *Social Science Information*, **42** (3): 293–337.

Etzkowitz, Henry, Andrew Webster, Christiane Gebhardt and Branca Regina Cantisano Terra (2000), 'The future of the university and the university of the future: evolution of ivory tower to entrepreneurial paradigm', *Research Policy*, **29** (2): 313–30.

Heher, Anthony D. (2006), 'Return on investment in innovation: implications for institutions and national agencies', *Journal of Technology Transfer*, **31** (4): 403–14.

Higher Education Evaluation and Accreditation Council of Taiwan (HEEACT) (2008), 'Performance ranking of scientific papers by world universities', http://ranking.heeact.edu.tw.

ISI – Essential Science Indicators Database.

ISI Web of Science Database.

Lee, Chong-Moon, William F. Miller, Marguerite Gong Hancock and Henry S. Rowen (eds) (2000), *The Silicon Valley Edge: A Habitat for Innovation and Entrepreneurship*, Stanford, CA: Stanford University Press.

National University of Singapore (NUS) (Various years), *Annual Report*, Singapore: NUS.

National University of Singapore (NUS) (Various years), *NUS Research Report*, Singapore: NUS Office of Research.

Saxenian, Annalee (2000), *Silicon Valley's New Immigrant Entrepreneurs*, San Francisco: Public Policy Institute of California.

Saxenian, Annalee (2002), *Local and Global Networks of Immigrant Professionals in Silicon Valley*, San Francisco: Public Policy Institute of California.

Shane, Scott (2004), *Academic Entrepreneurship: University Spin-offs and Wealth Creation*, Cheltenham, UK and Northampton, MA, USA: Edward Elgar.

United States Patent and Trademark Office (USPTO) Database of Issued Patents website: http://patft.uspto.gov/.

Wong, Poh-Kam (2006), 'The re-making of Singapore's high tech enterprise eco-system', in H. Rowen, W. Miller and M. Hancock (eds), *Making IT: The Rise of Asia in High Tech.*, Stanford, CA: Stanford University Press, pp. 123–74.

Wong, Poh-Kam and Yuen-Ping Ho (2007), 'Knowledge sources of innovation in a small open economy: the case of Singapore', *Scientometrics*, **70** (2): 223–49.

Wong, Poh-Kam, Yuen-Ping Ho and Annette Singh (2007), 'Towards an "Entrepreneurial University" model to support knowledge-based economic development: the Case of the National University of Singapore', *World Development*, **35** (6), 914–59.

Wong, Poh-Kam, Lena Lee, Yuen-Ping Ho and Finna Wong (2005), *Global Entrepreneurship Monitor 2004: Singapore Report*, Singapore: National University of Singapore Entrepreneurship Centre.

Wong, Poh-Kam and Annette Singh (2008), 'From technology adopter to innovator: the dynamics of change in the national system of innovation in Singapore', in C. Edquist and L. Hommen (eds), *Small Economy Innovation Systems: Comparing Globalization, Change and Policy in Asia and Europe*, Cheltenham, UK and Northampton, MA, USA: Edward Elgar, pp. 71–112.

8. University-based entrepreneurship ecosystems: key success factors and recommendations

Mark P. Rice, Michael L. Fetters and Patricia G. Greene

Three overarching findings emerged from our analysis of the long histories of the six university-based entrepreneurship ecosystems (U-BEEs) in this book:

- Finding 1. There are alternative pathways to the development of a comprehensive, highly evolved university-based entrepreneurship ecosystem.
- Finding 2. Although the relative strengths of the elements of their U-BEES may vary, all cases share common elements.
- Finding 3. The six case studies reveal success factors for the development of a comprehensive U-BEE that will be illuminating for universities that wish to pursue development of their own ecosystems.

Throughout the discussion of these findings, we highlight key passages from the previous six chapters.

PATHWAYS FOR DEVELOPMENT OF UNIVERSITY-BASED ENTREPRENEURSHIP ECOSYSTEMS

Where the development of U-BEEs leads is clear: to an extraordinarily resource-rich, comprehensive and dynamic context for delivering entrepreneurship education and for supporting the start-up and development of new ventures. However the development pathways for each of the U-BEEs showcased in this book varied. As stated by Kathleen Allen and Mark Lieberman of the University of Southern California (USC):

> There is no one best way to create an entrepreneurship ecosystem. In our experience, it is a multi-stage process where the stages are not clearly defined as the

university moves through them. Each stage develops relationships and capabilities that enable the ecosystem to evolve to the next level.

At Babson the starting point was a single for-credit course, followed relatively quickly by three flagship programs: the Academy of Distinguished Entrepreneurs (1978), the Babson College Entrepreneurship Research Conference (1980) and the Symposium of Entrepreneurship Educators. Over time, integration of entrepreneurship into the core curriculum, a proliferation of electives and specializations, and innovation in pedagogy established a robust learning environment. In the past decade (2000–2009), Babson has engaged in a dramatic increase in global research programs and globalization with respect to partnerships.

Key start-up activities for the EM Lyon U-BEE included the integration of entrepreneurship into the school curriculum in the early 1980s, the founding of the Entrepreneurship Center in 1984, and the establishment of the Enterprise Creation Chair in 1985 with the support of Lyonnaise de Banque.

The entrepreneurship ecosystem at the University of Southern California began its evolution in the 1960s when the first courses in entrepreneurship were offered. In the early 1970s USC launched a concentration in entrepreneurship at the graduate level and an Office of Technology Licensing. However the development of its U-BEE was dramatically accelerated by the endowment of its Entrepreneurship Center in 1997 with a $5 million gift from Lloyd Greif.

At The University of Texas at Austin, a variety of early entrepreneurial initiatives emerged in the early 1980s, for example, the Moot Corp Competition in 1984. The development of the ecosystem accelerated in the late 1980s, when the IC² Institute implemented a strategy to pull government, businesses and academic institutions together to build technology-based firms. The Austin Technology Incubator was launched with the support of the legendary George Kozmetsky (former dean of the business school) and the RGK Foundation. It in turn spawned a variety of initiatives – including the Texas Capital Network – that built out The University of Texas at Austin ecosystem.

The U-BEE at Tecnológico de Monterrey started with a practicum for students who were starting businesses, and its major breakthrough came with the development of models for incubators and technology parks that have been widely adopted throughout Mexico.

Early milestones in the evolution of the National University of Singapore's U-BEE included the establishment of the Centre for Management of Innovation and Technopreneurship (CMIT) in 1988, and the founding of the NUS technology transfer office in 1992.

For a university just beginning the process of developing a U-BEE, where is the best place to start? The resource-based view of the firm – the theory that the basis for competitive advantage lies primarily in the application of the firm's bundle of differentiated and inimitable resources – provides the most useful starting point. Typically these resources include a sponsor (a university or community leader who is willing and able to proclaim an entrepreneurial vision) and an entrepreneurial champion within the university community (usually a member of the administration or faculty). These entrepreneurial leaders will often create a pilot program – an initial course, a research initiative or an outreach program – in order to gain visibility, attract additional talent and acquire resources, for example from donors, sponsors in the business community and government agencies.

Success in a pilot project leads to the start-up of additional initiatives, and often the ecosystem grows organically until it reaches a critical mass. At that point, it will likely become part of the university's formal strategic planning and budgeting process.

It is also possible that the catalyst for starting this process is market pull. For example students may push for a course in entrepreneurship or a forum for networking with successful entrepreneurs. Alumni of the university who have been successful entrepreneurs may lobby the university to establish entrepreneurship initiatives, and they may also be willing to provide financial support and advice to help get the new programs started. A government agency may champion an economic development program and solicit the support of the university.

Regardless of how the U-BEE development process starts, typically internal and external forces act to encourage (or in some cases inhibit) the development of the U-BEE. If successful, the development process will result in a robust curricular and co-curricular program for the development of entrepreneurial talent, a dynamic set of research initiatives that create a flow of intellectual property, and a comprehensive set of outreach programs that create a resource-rich environment in which entrepreneurship can flourish.

ELEMENTS OF UNIVERSITY-BASED ENTREPRENEURSHIP ECOSYSTEMS

An entrepreneurship ecosystem provides a resource-rich environment that enhances the development of nascent entrepreneurial talent and the rate of start-up, survival and success of new ventures. Over an extended period of time, a minimum of 20 years, the U-BEEs showcased herein accumulated an impressive array of courses, outreach programs, research initiatives, people and resources. It is important to note that this accumulation process did not occur overnight as a consequence of a major one-time gift or a singular one-time commitment of budgetary resources by the host university. Table 8.1 records the elements of each university's entrepreneurship ecosystem.

Although the six universities share many of the same components, local conditions drive differentiation among the elements, organizational structure and sources of financing of the U-BEEs. For example universities whose main objective is enhancing technology transfer are likely to have much more robust and active technology transfer offices and more involved science and engineering schools in developing the U-BEE. Universities in countries with a strong culture of philanthropy are more likely to have endowed chairs as magnets for donations, whereas universities in countries where the government is the major driver of economic development may acquire more of the funding for developing and sustaining the U-BEE from regional, state or national government agencies. Table 8.1 is not meant to serve as a checklist for the development of U-BEE elements. Instead it reflects the reality that U-BEEs will vary in some of the details as a function of strategic objectives, gaps being addressed through the U-BEE, availability of financial resources and expertise, leadership preferences, and so forth.

Is it imperative to engage and sustain most or all of the elements listed in Table 8.1 in order to have an entrepreneurship ecosystem? The answer is no; however a critical mass of these elements must be achieved to sustain a flow of nascent entrepreneurs and nascent entrepreneurial ventures. For some U-BEEs, evidence of a relatively high flow rate of nascent entrepreneurs and nascent entrepreneurial ventures may be the primary metric of success. (It is possible that a significant percentage of the nascent entrepreneurs and entrepreneurial ventures may opt to relocate to an even more evolved entrepreneurship ecosystem to pursue new opportunities and to enhance growth rate.) In other cases, the strategic intent of the university sponsor of the U-BEE may extend to contributing to regional economic development, specifically to support the start-up, survival and growth of entrepreneurial ventures. For these universities, economic impact may be another important success metric, often operationalized as the rate of job creation or the growth rate of revenues aggregated across the ventures that have emerged within the entrepreneurship ecosystem. For the university sponsors of yet other U-BEEs, technology transfer is a primary driver, and for these U-BEEs, the rate of production of patents and licensing revenue may be important metrics of success, along with the rate of start-up, survival and growth of new technological ventures that are vehicles for technology commercialization.

Table 8.1   Elements of university-based entrepreneurship ecosystems

Elements of U-BEE	Babson	EM Lyon	USC	UT-Austin	Tecnológico de Monterrey	NUS
Senior leadership sponsorship	Yes	Yes	Yes	Yes	Yes	Yes
Strategic vision	Yes	Yes	Yes	Yes	Yes	Yes
Entrepreneurship academic division	Yes	No	Yes*	No	Yes	No
Entrepreneurship course	Yes	Yes	Yes	Yes	Yes	Yes
Entrepreneurship practicum	Yes	Yes	Yes	Yes	Yes	Yes
Entrepreneurship concentration or minor	Yes	Yes	Yes	Yes	Yes	Yes
Entrepreneurship courses for non-business majors	Yes	Yes	Yes	Yes	Yes	Yes
Ongoing curriculum innovation	Yes	Yes	Yes	Yes	Yes	Yes
Entrepreneurship research program or center	Yes	Yes	Yes	Yes	No	Yes
Entrepreneurship center	Yes	Yes	Yes	Yes	Yes	Yes
Networking events	Yes	Yes	Yes	Yes	Yes	Yes
Entrepreneurship student club(s)	Yes	No	Yes	Yes	Yes	No
Business plan competition(s)	Yes	Yes	Yes	Yes	Yes	Yes
Student venture investment fund	Yes	No	No	No	No	Yes
Links to angel and venture funds	Yes	Yes	Yes	Yes	Yes	Yes
Incubator	Yes	Yes	Yes**	Yes	Yes	Yes

Table 8.1   (continued)

Elements of U-BEE	Babson	EM Lyon	USC	UT-Austin	Tecnológico de Monterrey	NUS
Entrepreneurship endowed chair(s)	Yes	No	Yes	Yes	Yes	No
Center or program endowment	Yes	No	Yes	Yes	No	No

Notes:
*   With Entrepreneurship Center.
**   With local incubator.

In theory it is possible for a university sponsor to create a significant number of the programs listed in Table 8.1 and yet not catalyze the creation of enough nascent entrepreneurs and entrepreneurial ventures to achieve success. Why? The university and the region in which it is located may not have nor be able to attract enough entrepreneurial talent. All the elements listed above contribute to the creation of a favorable context for entrepreneurship, but the outcomes will be limited if there are too few entrepreneurs to take advantage of the favorable context. For this reason, it is important for a U-BEE to seek out and cultivate entrepreneurial talent, typically starting with students and alumni and then extending to faculty, staff and local entrepreneurs who have no previous affiliation with the university.

Similarly, unless there are sufficient financial resources, it will be difficult to achieve significant regional economic impact. The U-BEE may be able to catalyze a flow of nascent entrepreneurs and entrepreneurial ventures, but those who are committed to growth are likely to flow out of the region. Those ventures that remain in the region will not require growth capital because they start and remain small and are therefore able to self-finance. Creating the critical mass of elements of a U-BEE, therefore, means that sufficient flows of talent, ideas and resources – and the connections within and among the flows – must be catalyzed. Chapter 7, which focuses on the National University of Singapore's U-BEE, illuminates this dilemma by highlighting Singapore's need to overcome four transformational challenges.

The first was a requirement to shift Singapore's capabilities from using technology towards creating technology. As Singapore moves towards a knowledge-based economy, it will need to achieve a more balanced national innovation system that emphasizes both attracting foreign multinationals to bring more innovative activities to Singapore and developing local innovation capabilities through greater public investment in R&D.

The second challenge is that Singapore still lacks a sufficient number of skilled knowledge professionals, especially research scientists and engineers. This is a major constraint to the development of its national innovation system since a critical mass of science and technology manpower is needed for its high-tech industrial drive, especially in the life sciences.

The third challenge is the continued need for a more entrepreneurial culture and mindset among Singaporeans. Instead a culture that eschews risk and failure has developed over the years, and entrepreneurship has not generally been considered a viable career option.

The fourth challenge is that the innovation system in Singapore has a relatively underdeveloped technology commercialization ecosystem. There are not enough private enterprises capable of taking research and development (R&D) from public research institutes and universities and developing product or process innovations in the marketplace. The venture ecosystem for supporting new start-ups is also weak. The VC industry is in the early stage of development in Singapore, and the established VC funds tend to focus on less risky later-stage financing. A critical mass of sophisticated business angel investors is needed, along with the dense social networks of venture professionals, mentors and deal-making institutions (start-up law firms, serial entrepreneurs, and so on) that characterize places like Silicon Valley.

These four challenges identified for Singapore reflect the need for a cadre of innovators and entrepreneurs plus the ecosystem (particularly sources of capital and expertise) that enhances the prospects for their success.

SEVEN KEY SUCCESS FACTORS

As we reviewed the evolution and elements of the six U-BEE case studies, insights emerged about their success factors. From those insights, we developed recommendations for other universities starting down the path of developing a robust U-BEE.

Success Factor 1: Senior Leadership Vision, Engagement and Sponsorship

In all six universities one of the keys to sustaining the commitment to build a robust entrepreneurship ecosystem has been the engagement of senior leadership, typically at the dean and/or presidential level and through a succession of entrepreneurial senior leaders. An important part of that engagement has been the declaration of strategic intent, namely that entrepreneurship is a central part of the vision of the university and of the university's role in the extended community. In addition, the senior leader proactively advocates for entrepreneurship within the host university and with individuals, government, media, other academic institutions and the business community – wherever there may be sources of financial and non-financial support. Senior leaders enhance commitment, serve as advocates and energize stakeholders when they publicly recognize and celebrate the successes that occur along the development path.

In the mid-1970s Babson's new president, Ralph K. Sorenson, was trying to deepen his understanding of Babson's identity: how to use or change it to differentiate Babson from other schools and in the process revolutionize business education. He reasoned that Babson could not compete head-to-head with the well-known universities in the Boston area, but as he studied Babson's history he saw that its founder, Roger Babson, had been an entrepreneur, as had numerous Babson alumni who had started and managed successful new ventures. He also met a management professor, Jack Hornaday, who wanted to teach entrepreneurship from a human behavior perspective and had added a segment on entrepreneurs to one of his courses. This strand of entrepreneurship running through Babson's DNA showed the way to building a unique new identity.

The emphasis on entrepreneurship at EM Lyon emerged under the leadership of Philippe Albert in the 1980s. In 2003 Patrick Molle, president of EM Lyon Business School, formalized and updated the centrality of entrepreneurship by launching the Educating Entrepreneurs for the World initiative.

The evolution of the U-BEE at USC has been more organic and bottom-up than what the other five schools experienced. Even so the U-BEE champions there believe that a commitment at the highest levels to support innovation and entrepreneurship and make it critical to the school's mission is essential to the success of an ecosystem. USC President Sample's leadership and vision, dating from his inauguration in 1991, have always included these elements, and they are also reflected in the number of entrepreneurs that Sample has recruited to the USC board of trustees.

The concept of the technopolis framework, a paradigm of technology-driven economic development, was pioneered at the IC^2 Institute at the University of Texas at Austin. The concept emphasized interlocking relationships among academia, business and government. In a Harvard Business School case on this topic, Austin was called 'Kozmetsky's Technopolis', a reference to the former dean of the business school at The University of Texas at Austin, George Kozmetsky, who at that time was the founder and director of the IC^2 Institute.

Promulgated in February 2005, the vision statement of the senior leadership at Tecnológico de Monterrey declared that by 2015 the school should be 'the leading educational institution in Latin America' in the 'generation of business management and incubation models'. To fulfill its institutional vision for 2015, Tecnológico de Monterrey has developed high-value programs and infrastructure to spur technology-based enterprise development.

Singapore born and United States trained, C.F. Shih came to the National University of Singapore in 1997 as deputy vice-chancellor and in 2000 assumed the role of president. With strong support from the government, he provided crucial leadership that not only significantly accelerated the pace of change of several ongoing initiatives, but more importantly, initiated a strategic shift towards an entrepreneurial university model. As is typical of innovative leaders, he did so by establishing a new vision for the university that encompassed an explicit recognition of entrepreneurial development and by creating a new organizational vehicle to spearhead change towards the new vision.

Recommendation 1

It is highly unlikely that a university will be able to create a U-BEE without the sponsorship of a senior leader. In many cases, it is the president or dean who initiates the development of the U-BEE. When the process is initiated by a member of the faculty or a program leader, the champion needs to secure the support of the appropriate senior leader. When the process is initiated by a supporter of the university (a government agency or a key donor), support for entrepreneurship should be one of the criteria for hiring the senior academic leader to whom the activity will report.

Success Factor 2: Strong Programmatic and Faculty Leadership

In all six U-BEEs showcased in this book, strong administrative leadership in entrepreneurship programs, centers, projects and initiatives and strong faculty leadership with respect to teaching, research and outreach have been critical to the evolution of the ecosystem. The authors and editors of the chapters in this book have all played one or more of these roles within their U-BEEs. And we can all identify the predecessor champions who created the foundation on which we continue to build our U-BEEs. A single, highly capable and driven individual may be able to champion a specific program, course or research initiative, but it takes a team of people skilled in program development and program management;

curriculum development, pedagogy and teaching; collaborative research; and relationship-building inside and outside the university to create an entrepreneurship ecosystem.

Recommendation 2

Some faculty members will opt to fulfill the traditional expectations of focusing on research, teaching and institutional service, all of which make important contributions to the creation of a dynamic, high-impact learning environment. Faculty who opt for this professional pattern need to be complemented by faculty and staff who are institution builders by nature, inclination and capabilities. Universities that strive to develop a U-BEE need people who excel in both categories. To some extent it is easier to recruit and support the traditional faculty. After all, they do what they have been trained to do. Developing a cadre of individuals in the second category is more challenging. To be effective, they need to have credibility as members of the faculty, but they must also have the skills required for program development and management. Any university pursuing the development of a U-BEE needs to be proactive in the recruitment, development and retention of faculty and administrative leaders who are innovative and entrepreneurial, and who will drive the creation, development, management and ongoing renewal of the U-BEE. Furthermore the university needs to manage the flow of talent continually throughout the U-BEE evolutionary process.

Success Factor 3: Sustained Commitment over a Long Period of Time

Often impassioned leaders or donors hope that the pathway to a robust entrepreneurship ecosystem can be relatively short. Our conviction is that building such an ecosystem requires intensity of commitment, diligence, skill and significant resources, all of them applied over the course of decades. The development processes for the six U-BEEs described in Chapters 2–7 have taken in excess of 20 years. In each case the process was neither linear nor did it unfold at a uniform rate. In some phases, leadership has been more committed and at other times less committed (or distracted), but in all cases continuity of leadership has been sustained by one or more champions or sponsors. Resources have generally been insufficient to undertake and accomplish everything the champions envisioned, but in each case the champions have been skillful and reasonably successful in attracting resources. Some elements of the ecosystem have waned while others have emerged, but overall the ecosystems have become stronger with time. The starting points for the decades-long evolutionary path for each of the U-BEE case studies are highlighted below.

Babson

While Babson's focus on business education was established at the start, the entrepreneurial approach was increasingly emphasized over the years. Babson's first entrepreneurship course was offered in 1968, and in 1977 the mission of Babson College under President Ralph Sorenson was changed to focus explicitly on the entrepreneurial aspects of the college.

EM Lyon

The school's foray into entrepreneurship training in the 1980s and 90s led to a substantial body of expertise among the school staff. Some of the key professors involved in teaching entrepreneurship to undergraduate and graduate students became the core team of entrepreneur trainers in the early days of the venture creation program.

USC

The entrepreneurship ecosystem at USC began its evolution in the 1960s with the first graduate courses dedicated to helping students understand the mindset and skills required to launch new businesses.

The University of Texas at Austin

Early research at the IC^2 Institute centered on institutional arrangements for new linkages among government, business and academia. The major research task of the IC^2 Institute in 1979 was to determine how society could build confidence, cooperation and collaboration among major institutions, especially for the purpose of economic growth and job creation based on commercializing science and technology.

Tecnológico de Monterrey

Tecnológico de Monterrey established its entrepreneurship program in 1978 through a small group of professors and business people who, as a committee, guided a group of students through the process of starting a business.

NUS

The Centre for Management of Innovation and Technopreneurship (CMIT) was originally established in 1988 to serve the university. In 2001 it became a division of NUS Enterprise and was renamed the NUS Entrepreneurship Centre (NEC).

Recommendation 3

For the U-BEE development process to extend across decades, continuity of support from senior leaders and program champions is critical. Therefore succession planning at the level of the university, the school, the division, centers and programs should take this into account. Long-term commitment of financial resources – in the form of either endowments or set-in-stone, multiyear budgetary commitments – likewise reinforces and supports leadership support. U-BEE sponsors and champions can increase the probability of sustained university commitment by securing long-term financial commitments since the providers of those resources will be able to influence succession planning to ensure continuity and competence of leadership.

Success Factor 4: Commitment of Substantial Financial Resources

Committing substantial financial resources to the U-BEE development process increases the probability of success in two ways. First, it reduces the time and energy expended by sponsors and champions in a constant scramble to secure ongoing funding. Second, it insulates the U-BEE development process from the resistance or obstructionism that may arise in other parts of the university. Each of the six U-BEEs in this book acquired long-term financial support, typically from multiple sources. Some examples are provided below.

Babson
At Babson transformative gifts have included Arthur M. Blank's endowment in the late 1990s for the Center for Entrepreneurship named in his honor and more recently a $10.8 million gift from the Lewis Charitable Foundation for the establishment of an institute to support teaching, research and outreach in social entrepreneurship.

EM Lyon
The annual budget for entrepreneurship activities at EM Lyon of approximately €1.5 million is covered by the Entrepreneurs for the World foundation in tandem with funding from private companies and public funds. The share of private financing is over 60 percent

USC
The $5 million endowment of the Greif Center at the Marshall School in 1997 has been a critical building block in establishing a foundation for sustaining the USC U-BEE. It gave the program an annual operating budget

that enabled it to fund a number of new programs and events. In the following year, a $100 million endowment gift to the School on Engineering catalyzed a partnership with the Greif Center that six years later resulted in the establishment of the USC Technology Commercialization Alliance (now the USC Marshall Center for Technology Commercialization), a multischool collaboration that has become the central source for faculty, researchers and students of information, research, education and services related to the commercialization of USC technology through entrepreneurship.

NUS
When President Shih launched NUS Enterprise Centre, he committed an annual operating budget equivalent to about 1 percent of the university's overall budget.

Recommendation 4

It is unlikely that a U-BEE will be sustainable if the sponsors and champions must constantly struggle to secure the resources necessary to survive. This does not mean that the sponsors and champions will ever be relieved of the responsibility to pursue additional resources in order to support new innovation initiatives and sustain programs whose costs will rise with inflation. A university committed to developing a successful and sustainable U-BEE must have sufficient long-term funding from endowments, grants and secure budget commitments so that the U-BEE will not struggle for survival. Furthermore the university and the champions of the U-BEE must aggressively and continuously pursue additional resources.

Success Factor 5: Commitment to Continuing Innovation in Curriculum and Programs

It is all too easy for the sponsors and champions who inherit the responsibility for a U-BEE from previous leaders to settle for sustaining what others have started. However the context in which U-BEEs operate is constantly changing and U-BEEs need to lead or respond to that change. From a portfolio perspective, some of the elements of a U-BEE will need to be sustained, some will need to be enhanced, and some will need to be diminished or eliminated. Furthermore any U-BEE that hopes to continue to lead must constantly innovate by developing new initiatives, some of which will take hold and others that will not. In each of the six U-BEEs described in this book, there are numerous examples of continuing innovation. It is important for senior leaders to adopt a portfolio model that supports continual innovation, recognizes and celebrates successes and provides cover for champions when innovative initiatives do not pan out.

Babson

Even though they have undergone significant and important changes, by and large the building blocks put in place in the 1980s have remained an important part of the foundation of Babson's U-BEE: the Babson College Entrepreneurship Research Conference, the Symposium for Entrepreneurship Educators, the Academy of Distinguished Entrepreneurs, and the entrepreneurship curriculum. However through Babson's continuing commitment to innovation, the Babson U-BEE has grown substantially since 1980. For example, with respect to research, the Global Entrepreneurship Monitor (GEM), the Successful Transgenerational Entrepreneurship Practices program (STEP), the Center for Women's Leadership research program, and the Diana Project, among other research initiatives, have dramatically expanded Babson's entrepreneurship research footprint.

EM Lyon

Like other U-BEEs, EM Lyon provides an incubation support system. The EM Lyon experience illustrates how innovation can occur within a well-established element of a U-BEE. The incubator in EM Lyon has been at the heart of all entrepreneurial activity. Since 1984 more than 600 companies and 10 000 jobs have been created there. The incubator has maintained strong links with internal teaching departments, entrepreneurship professors and researchers as well as with external entities that provide complementary and useful resources like funding, intellectual capital and networks. In June 2008, more than 20 years after its inception, the long-standing incubator was revitalized. Called the 'new-generation incubator', it now offers a longer-term and more highly structured set of support services, integrating four key services: teaching, coaching and mentoring, networking, and infrastructure aid.

USC

The chair of the Department of Electrical Engineering – Electrophysics in the Viterbi School of Engineering wanted to create awareness for the School of Engineering's new technology initiative and the new institute made possible by a $100 million endowment from entrepreneur Alfred Mann. To do so he began a collaboration with the Greif Center. That collaboration precipitated a six-year effort on the part of Kathleen Allen from the business school, George Bekey from the engineering school and others to establish the USC Technology Commercialization Alliance (TCA), which was recognized by the university and the deans of the schools of business, engineering and medicine. What started as a collaboration to discover mutual interests grew to include the USC College of Letters, Arts and Sciences and become the central source of information, research, education and services related to the commercialization of USC technology through entrepreneurship.

The University of Texas at Austin

Building on the international success of the Moot Corp business plan competition and the world-class research activities of the IC^2 Institute, The University of Texas at Austin has participated in creating a technopolis under the banner of the Austin model. IC^2 has launched the three primary alliances to support the formation of new technology ventures: the Austin Technology Incubator, the Texas Technology Incubator and the Texas Capital Network.

Tecnológico de Monterrey

Thanks to the experience of Tecnológico de Monterrey in distance-education models for the preparation, training and education of its students, graduates and community members, the virtual incubation format was defined in 2002 as a strategic part of the Business Incubator Network. This format relied on the Emprendetec portal, a technological tool that also supports the face-to-face incubation format. The Emprendetec portal was released in May 2003, thus making it possible for all the Tecnológico de Monterrey incubators to offer a virtual format to their users. Another example of the school's commitment to ongoing innovation addresses the need to enhance sources of capital for entrepreneurs. Tecnológico de Monterrey has been implementing a new strategy called Investment Clubs, through which it strives to stimulate the venture capital culture.

NUS

A classic example of curriculum innovation is the development and implementation of a Technopreneurship minor program open to all NUS undergraduates, but with a strong focus on science and engineering students. Developing a program to help technical students become more business-savvy and entrepreneurial-minded addressed a weakness in the existing educational programs of NUS. NUS Enterprise had initially asked the NUS business school to offer these courses to technical students, but the business school declined because it was uncertain that the demand would last. Although the NUS Entrepreneurship Centre was not an academic department, through the strong championing of NUS Enterprise it was granted a special academic teaching unit status by the provost so that it could offer the courses. By undertaking an active program of marketing that leveraged NEC's various non-classroom educational activities, NEC was able to increase enrolment rapidly in its Technopreneurship courses from fewer than 200 in the first year to over 1300 by 2005–06. When the program was found to be viable in 2007, its administration was transferred to the NUS Business School in 2007.

Recommendation 5

Continuing innovation must become a cultural norm for a university developing a U-BEE. Innovation should be explicitly identified as a component of the planning and management processes used to develop and sustain a U-BEE, and as a part of the performance measurement system for individuals and programs.

Success Factor 6: An Appropriate Organizational Infrastructure

Although the titles of the programs and organizational entities may vary, as do the scope of their activities, every U-BEE described in this book has organizational units that focus on: advancing and managing the initiatives in research (research centers, research programs and endowed chairs); teaching and curriculum development (entrepreneurship divisions, curriculum committees, case libraries, teacher development programs); and outreach (incubators, networking events, technology licensing offices, business plan competitions). In addition there are a variety of formal and informal organizational mechanisms for connecting the U-BEE to the overall mission of the school and to complementary internal and external partners.

The sponsors and champions of the U-BEE need to design the U-BEE organizational structure that is required to create the projected outcomes while taking into account conflicting pressures. The goal of minimizing costs associated with coordinating and communicating across multiple elements argues for simplicity; however the effectiveness of each element in achieving its objectives is served by focus. On the one hand, the goal of ongoing innovation argues for flexibility and fluidity. On the other hand, the need to defend the U-BEE in the face of challenges and opposition from traditional and entrenched parts of the university argues for operational excellence with respect to execution in organizational processes, and proactive and constructive engagement in interface management.

This is an appropriate place to acknowledge that entrepreneurship is in many ways misaligned with the traditional university that favors disciplinary purity and isolation, rewards the pursuit of knowledge for its own sake, and creates a barrier between scholarship and the application of knowledge to practice. Entrepreneurship is fundamentally cross-disciplinary and thrives in an environment of dynamic and fluid connections. It also requires skill and judgment to complement knowledge, which makes applied learning such a valuable part of the learning process supported by a U-BEE. Applied learning for students and support of new venturing activity is enhanced by connections with the business community, another key element of building a U-BEE. Naturally there are individuals and organizational units within universities that are uncomfortable with entrepreneurship and establishing links to business. They may actively oppose the development of a U-BEE and connections with the business community, favoring instead the traditional university model.

This problem is highlighted in the following excerpt from Chapter 4, which described the U-BEE at USC: 'The structural organization of the university into profit centers, for example, makes the cross-disciplinary collaboration needed for an effective ecosystem difficult at best. Concerns about sharing tuition revenues, faculty salaries and general expenses often create barriers that are difficult to overcome.'

Recommendation 6

Start with a small number of initiatives that are aligned with the rest of the organization and that clearly advance institutional priorities (for example fund-raising, recruiting students, outreach to the community). Focus on doing something well in order to create a foundation for success and growth. Identify the biggest needs of the host university (often development of entrepreneurial talent, which can be addressed through classroom and experiential learning) and address them first. Over time design, develop and implement organizational entities that can effectively focus resources (particularly talent and funding) on achieving key performance outcomes related to research, teaching and programs that support applied learning, network building, new venture creation, technology transfer and so forth.

Success Factor 7: Commitment to Building the Extended Enterprise and Achieving Critical Mass

A successful U-BEE will not only have a strong local impact but will also achieve global reach and impact, particularly through a global network of partner institutions. As mentioned earlier, one mark of success – in fact a requirement for success – is strong internal relationships with other faculty, divisions and schools. Also needed are strong local, national and global external relationships with the business community, the investment community, the alumni community, other universities, and non-governmental organizations (NGOs) and government agencies. Without this critical mass, a nascent ecosystem is vulnerable to the loss of a key person, to the waning of support because of new institutional leadership with different priorities, or to shrinking financial resources if the institution is confronted with financial distress. The more quickly a school moves past the pilot stage and involves multiple stakeholders, the more likely it is to create momentum and gain recognition as an important part of the university strategy. The creativity and energy of a portfolio of stakeholders builds momentum quickly and enhances the probability of sustained development. The six U-BEEs in this book have proactively developed an appropriate portfolio of activities and increased the scope of those activities, and over time have achieved a critical mass. Their reach, influence and impact have progressed from the host university to the region, to the nation and to the world.

Babson
By partnering with a wide variety of universities, NGOs and governments and through the collaborative research activities described previously (in particular, the Babson College Entrepreneurship Research Conference, the Global Entrepreneurship Monitor, the Successful Transgenerational Entrepreneurship Practices program and the Diana Project) and the Symposiums for Entrepreneurship Educators, Babson has developed global networks and delivered global impact. In 2009 Babson began pursuing the development of the Global Entrepreneurship Educators' Network.

EM Lyon
Numerous stakeholders – students, faculty, investors, entrepreneurs, school management, research centers, industry, community and regional representatives – have played a key role in the entrepreneurial ecosystem at EM Lyon.

USC
In terms of the relationship of the university nodes with the community and region, the primary areas of connection and collaboration are with alumni entrepreneurs, the LA Technology Business Center, local industries that support innovation at the university, and the angel and venture capital community.

The University of Texas at Austin
Building on its success in Austin, IC^2 is now helping sponsors around the world to implement and test the Austin model for the diffusion of science

to create wealth and jobs. Countries where scholars are measuring the effects of the model include China, the United Kingdom, India, Israel, Japan, Korea, Poland, Russia, Portugal, Iraq and the United States.

Tecnológico de Monterrey
Creating an entrepreneurial ecosystem involves more than the physical spaces where entrepreneurs interact. The space is important, but the ecosystem includes everything: alignment with institutional objectives; access to university resources such as laboratories, researchers and knowledge transfer; reorientation of research initiatives to become market driven; participation of the business community through business angel groups; participation of venture capital firms; involvement of municipal, state and federal governments in creating the necessary legal framework and supporting job creation and new companies.

NUS
To be successful the university must ultimately expand beyond its walls to stimulate regional entrepreneurship education and activity. This expansion strengthens the university's position as an entrepreneurship ecosystem hub as it acts as a magnetic force for all types of entrepreneurship activity: invention, new ventures, seed funding, later-stage funding, mentoring and ultimately a vibrant social network.

Recommendation 7

Achieving sufficient scope and impact for sustainability requires that the U-BEE has an expansive vision and a commitment to achieving significant outcomes locally, regionally, nationally and globally. To some extent this will be achieved through the quality and variety of its research, teaching and outreach programs. But like any other entrepreneurial venture, having a great product and delivery system is not enough for success in the marketplace; the product must be marketed and sold. In the context of a U-BEE this translates as the need for sponsors and champions who are effective communicators, institution builders, resource acquirers, networkers and boundary spanners.

A VISION FOR THE FUTURE

Given the challenges of today, the world needs more than ever the positive change exemplified by entrepreneurial thought and action. University-based entrepreneurship ecosystems are uniquely capable of developing entrepreneurial talent and providing a context where it can thrive. We believe that the success factors and recommendations derived from the experiences described in our six case studies provide a roadmap for the development of U-BEEs. We hope these examples of highly successful global university-based entrepreneurship ecosystems will inspire and guide potential sponsors of entrepreneurship ecosystems in other universities, government agencies, NGOs and technology transfer organizations. In some cases the entrepreneurship ecosystems may be university-based, and in others one or more universities may be partners with a non-university primary sponsor. We hope the emergence of a critical mass of U-BEEs globally will help the world address its challenges and the human race achieve its full potential.

Index

Abbreviations used in the volume:
EM Lyon – EM Lyon Business School
NUS – National University of Singapore
U-BEE – University-Based Entrepreneurship Ecosystems
USC – University of Southern California
UTA – University of Texas at Austin

Titles of publications are in *italics*.

Printed and bound by CPI Group (UK) Ltd, Croydon, CR0 4YY

23/04/2025

14660957-0001